SCIENCE FICTION READERS THEATRE

SCIENCE FICTION READERS THEATRE

Anthony D. Fredericks

2002
TEACHER IDEAS PRESS
Libraries Unlimited
A Division of Greenwood Publishing Group, Inc.
Westport, Connecticut

TEACHER IDEAS PRESS
88 Post Road West
Westport, CT 06881
1-800-225-5800
www.lu.com

Library of Congress Cataloging-in-Publication Data

Fredericks, Anthony D.
    Science fiction readers theatre / Anthony D. Fredericks.
        p. cm.
 Includes bibliographical references and index.
    ISBN 1-56308-929-7
    1. Readers' theater. 2. Drama in education. 3. Young adult drama,
American. 4. Science fiction plays, American. I. Title.
    PN2081.R4 F74 2002
    808.5'4--dc21

                                                    2002008274

All of the following books are available from Teacher Ideas Press (P.O. Box 5007, 88 Post Road West, Westport, CT 06881; 1-800-225-5800; http://www.lu.com/tips).

Frantic Frogs and Other Frankly Fractured Folktales for Readers Theatre. ISBN: 1-56308-174-1. 123 pages; $19.50.

Have you heard "Don't Kiss Sleeping Beauty, She's Got Really Bad Breath" or "The Brussels Sprouts Man (The Gingerbread Man's Unbelievably Strange Cousin)"? This resource (grades 4–8) offers 30 reproducible satirical scripts for rip-roaring dramatics. Side-splitting send-ups and wacky folktales are guaranteed to bring snickers, chuckles, and belly laughs into the classroom.

The Integrated Curriculum: Books for Reluctant Readers, Grades 2–5, 2d ed. ISBN: 0-87287-994-1. 220 pages; $22.50.

This book presents guidelines for using literature with reluctant readers. It contains more than 40 book units on titles carefully selected to motivate the most reluctant readers, such as *The Three Bears, The Salamander Room*, and *Sky Tree*. Each unit includes a summary, discussion questions that foster critical thinking, and cross-curricular extensions.

Investigating Natural Disasters Through Children's Literature: An Integrated Approach. ISBN: 1-56308-861-4. 196 pages; $26.50.

The perfect book for students fascinated by *The Perfect Storm*. Natural disasters enthrall with their potency, might, and devastation. Tap into students' inherent awe of storms, volcanic eruptions, hurricanes, earthquakes, tornadoes, floods, avalanches, landslides, and tsunamis to open their minds to the wonders and power of the natural world. Using quality children's literature as a springboard to learning, this guide extends the understanding of science concepts through short activities, longer projects, and adventures.

Involving Parents Through Children's Literature: P–K. ISBN: 1-56308-022-2. 86 pages; $15.00.

Involving Parents Through Children's Literature: Grades 1–2. ISBN: 1-56308-012-5. 95 pages; $14.50.

Involving Parents Through Children's Literature: Grades 3–4. ISBN: 1-56308-013-3. 96 pages; $15.50.

Involving Parents Through Children's Literature: Grades 5–6. ISBN: 1-56308-014-1. 107 pages; $16.00.

This series of four books encourages parent participation in the learning process. Reproducible activity sheets based upon quality children's books are designed in a convenient format so children can take them home. Each sheet includes a book summary, discussion questions, and engaging activities for adults and children that stimulate comprehension and promote reading enjoyment.

The Librarian's Complete Guide to Involving Parents Through Children's Literature: Grades K–6. ISBN: 1-56308-538-0. 137 pages; $24.50.

Activities for 101 children's books are presented in a reproducible format, so librarians can distribute them to students to take home and share with parents. Each sheet includes a book summary, discussion questions, and a list of learning activities for parents to do with their children. These projects build strong bonds of communication between parents and children.

More Social Studies Through Children's Literature: An Integrated Approach. ISBN: 1-56308-761-8. 225 pages; $27.50.

Energize your social studies curriculum with dynamic, "hands-on, minds-on" projects based on such great children's books as *Amazing Grace*, *Fly Away Home*, and *Lon Po Po*. This book offers hundreds of activities designed to engage students in positive learning and help teachers implement national (and many state) standards. Each of the 33 units has book summaries, social studies topic areas, critical thinking questions, and dozens of easy-to-do activities for every grade level. This book is a perfect compliment to the earlier *Social Studies Through Children's Literature: An Integrated Approach* and effectively builds upon the success of that volume.

Readers Theatre for American History. ISBN: 1-56308-860-6. 178 pages; $30.00.

This book offers a participatory approach to American history. The 25 scripts allows students to become active participants in several historical events. Students will work alongside Father Junipero Serra at Mission san Juan Capistrano, they'll stand alongside Thomas Jefferson as he drafts the Declaration of Independence, they'll travel with a Midwestern family as they trek across the Oregon Trail, and they will experience Neal Armstrong's history-making trip to the moon. In short, students will get a "you are there" perspective to the unfolding of critical milestones and memorable circumstances that have shaped the American experience.

Science Adventures with Children's Literature: A Thematic Approach. ISBN: 1-56308-417-1. 190 pages; $24.50.

Focusing on the new Science Education Standards, this activity-centered resource uses a wide variety of children's literature to integrate science across the elementary curriculum. With a thematic approach, it features the best in science trade books; stimulating "hands-on, minds-on" activities and experiments in life, physical, Earth, and space sciences; and a host of tips, ideas, and strategies that make teaching and learning science an adventure. A delightful array of creative suggestions, dynamic thematic units in all areas of science, and stimulating new science literature and activities highlight this resource.

Science Discoveries on the Net: An Integrated Approach. ISBN: 1-56308-823-1. 315 pages; $27.50.

This book is designed to help teachers integrate the Internet into their science programs and enhance the scientific discoveries of students. The 88 units emphasize key concepts—based on national and state standards—throughout the science curriculum. Each unit is divided into five sections: Introduction (which includes basic background information on a topic), Research Questions (for students to investigate), Web Sites (the most current Internet sites on a topic), Children's Literature (the best books about a subject), and Activities (a host of "hands-on, minds-on" projects). The units are designed to energize any science curriculum and any classroom program.

Silly Salamanders and Other Slightly Stupid Stuff for Readers Theatre. ISBN: 1-56308-825-8. 161 pages; $23.50.

The third entry in the "wild and wacky" readers theatre trilogy is just as crazy and weird as the first two. How about these stories: "Snow White and the Seven Vertically Challenged Men," "The Big Bad Salamander and the Three Little Pigs," and "King Arthur and the Knights of the Polygon Table." This unbelievable resource offers students in grades 3–6 dozens of silly send-ups of well-known fairy tales, legends, and original stories guaranteed to fill any classroom with peels of laughter, howls of delight, and incredible language arts activities. It's a guaranteed winner!

Social Studies Discoveries on the Net: An Integrated Approach. ISBN:1-56308-824-X. 276 pages; $26.00.

This book is designed to help teachers integrate the Internet into their social studies programs and enhance the classroom discoveries of students. The 75 units emphasize key concepts—based on national and state standards—throughout the social studies curriculum. Each unit is divided into five sections: Introduction (which includes basic background information on a topic), Research Questions (for students to investigate), Web Sites (the most current Internet sites on a topic), Children's Literature (the best books about a subject), and Activities (a host of "hands-on, minds-on" projects).

Social Studies Through Children's Literature: An Integrated Approach. ISBN: 0-87287-970-4. 192 pages; $24.00.

Each of the 32 instructional units in this resource uses an activity-centered approach to elementary social studies, featuring children's picture books such as *Ox-Cart Man*, *In Coal Country*, and *Jambo Means Hello*. Each unit contains a book summary, social studies topic areas, curricular perspectives, critical thinking questions, and a large section of activities.

Tadpole Tales and Other Totally Terrific Titles for Readers Theatre. ISBN: 1-56308-547-X. 115 pages; $18.50.

A follow-up volume to the best selling *Frantic Frogs and Other Frankly Fractured Folktales for Readers Theatre*, this book provides primary level readers (grades 1–4) with a humorous assortment of wacky tales based on well-known Mother Goose rhymes. For example, "Old MacDonald Had a Farm and, Boy, Did It Stink (E-I-E-I-O)." More than 30 scripts and dozens of classroom extensions will keep your students rolling in the aisles.

CONTENTS

Part V: Future World

When I was growing up in West Los Angeles, my friends and I loved to watch science fiction movies. Every weekend, we would beg or borrow a dollar from our parents, hop on our bikes, and ride down to the local movie theatre to see the latest creature feature, scary movie, or alien invasion of Earth. This was, of course, in the days when a dollar would get you into a theatre *and* pay for popcorn and a soda. This was also in the days when Saturday afternoon matinees meant two movies, not just one. So, we could watch *It Came From Beneath the Sea* along with *The Day the Earth Stood Still*. Or, we could watch Steve McQueen and his teenage friends contend with *The Blob* and Vincent Price metamorphose into *The Fly* all in the same afternoon.

After the Saturday afternoon matinee, my friends and I would slowly pedal back to the neighborhood describing the realism of the latest monster movie or detailing how we would have vanquished the outer space visitors if we were in charge of the world. Depending on the movie, our conversations might go on for days about the creatures, aliens, or monsters we had seen and the ones we hoped to see in the future.

The power of those movies was so intense that they affected our lives with considerable impact. In fact, I'll never forget the first time my parents took me to San Francisco. As we crossed the Golden Gate Bridge headed toward Sausalito, I kept glancing around for the sucker marks left by the creature in *It Came From Beneath the Sea*. I was sure I had seen them and did everything I could to convince my sisters that the creature had, indeed, been wrapped around the southern end of the bridge.

For me, science fiction was very much a part of my youth. Those movies creatively stimulated my friends and I as no video game today ever could do. We traveled to distant planets, faced unspeakable horrors, fought vile and disgusting creatures, and were inundated with strange sights and images of weird beings as the fate of the world was decided in the space of 100 minutes or less. We were mesmerized and excited as we watched the possibilities of *what if* as opposed to *what is*.

To this day—at the high end of middle age—I cannot walk past a video store without a peek at some of the latest science fiction films. By the same token, I frequently find myself in the aisles of that same video store looking for some of the great science fiction classics of all time—such movies as *Them*, *The Day the Earth Stood Still*, *The Thing*, and *The Creature from the Black Lagoon*. I still remember the thrills I got from those movies as a child and more importantly, the ways in which my imagination would soar on endless flights of fancy.

This book offers your students a host of science fiction readers theatre scripts that will heighten their imaginations, stimulate their creativity, and actively engage them in a recognized and respected genre of literature. *Science Fiction Readers Theatre* presents readers theatre scripts that give students the chance to become actors in imaginative possibilities and creative impossibilities. Through these scripts, students will travel to distant worlds, discover the hideous secret of a new teacher, seek out the mysterious creature that lurks just around the corner, and fight off an insidious invader. In short, students will become travelers into a universe of creativity, imagination, and suspended disbelief that is without limits and without barriers.

Within these pages is a dynamic variety of creative learning possibilities for your intermediate-level classroom (grades 4 through 8). Here, your students will discover a fascinating collection of mind-expanding and imagination-building experiences—experiences that will reshape their perceptions of what creativity can be. Readers theatre offers opportunities to take unbelievable journeys through time, through space, and into the farthest reaches of the human mind. Be prepared for lots of action, lots of drama, and lots of fun! Let the adventures begin!

Tony Fredericks

What Is Readers Theatre?

Readers theatre is a storytelling device that stimulates the imagination and promotes *all* of the language arts. Simply stated, it is an oral interpretation of a piece of literature read in a dramatic style. Suzanne Barchers, an author of several readers theatre books, states that "…the primary focus in readers theatre is on an effective reading of the script rather than on a…memorized presentation….The ease of incorporating readers theatre into the language arts program offers teachers an exciting way to enhance that program, especially in today's classrooms that emphasize a variety of reading and listening experiences." (Barchers, 1993).

Simply put, readers theatre is an act of involvement, an opportunity to share, a time to creatively interact with others, and a personal interpretation of what can be or could be. In fact, readers theatre holds the promise of helping students understand and appreciate the richness of language, the interpretation of language, and how language can be a powerful vehicle for the comprehension and appreciation of different forms of literature. Readers theatre provides numerous opportunities for youngsters to make stories and literature come alive and pulsate with their own unique brand of perception and vision. In so doing, literature becomes personal and reflective and children have a breadth of opportunities to be authentic users of language.

What Is the Value of Readers Theatre?

I like to think of readers theatre as a way to actively engage in literature without the constraints of skills, memorization, or artificial structures (e.g., props, costumes, elaborate staging, etc.). Readers theatre allows children to breathe life and substance into literature—an interpretation that is neither right nor wrong, because it will be colored by kids' unique perspectives, experiences, and vision. It is, in fact, the readers' interpretation of a story that is intrinsically more valuable than some predetermined and/or preordained "translation" (something that might be found in a teacher's manual or curriculum guide, for example).

With that in mind, I'd like to share with you some of the many values I see in readers theatre:

- It stimulates curiosity and enthusiasm for literature. It allows children to experience different genres in a supportive and non-threatening format that underscores their active involvement.

- It allows children many different interpretations of the same story and facilitates the development of critical and creative thinking. There is no such thing as a right or wrong interpretation of a story; readers theatre validates that assumption.

- It focuses on all of the language arts—reading, writing, speaking, and listening. It supports a holistic philosophy of instruction and allows children to become responsible learners—ones who seek out answers to their own self-initiated inquiries.

- Because it is the performance that drives readers theatre, students are given more opportunities to invest themselves and their personalities in the production. The same story may be subject to several different presentations depending on the group or the individuals involved. As such, students learn that readers theatre can be explored in a host of ways.

- Students are given numerous opportunities to learn about the components of selected genres. This is particularly true when they are provided with opportunities to design and construct their own readers theatre scripts and have unlimited opportunities to discover the wide variations that can be used with a single piece.

- It is a participatory event. The characters as well as the audience are intimately involved in the design, structure, and delivery of the story. As such, students begin to realize that learning is not a solitary activity, but one that can be shared and discussed with others.

- It is informal and relaxed and does not require elaborate props, scenery, or costumes. It can be set up in any classroom or library. It does not require large sums of money, and it can be "put on" in any kind of environment— formal or informal.

- It stimulates the imagination and the creation of visual images. It has been substantiated that when children are provided with opportunities to create their own mental images, their comprehension and appreciation of a piece of writing is enhanced considerably. Because only a modicum of formal props and "set up" are required for any readers theatre production, the participants and audience members are encouraged to create supplemental "props" in their minds—props that may be more elaborate and exquisite than those found in the most lavish of plays.

- It enhances the development of cooperative learning strategies by requiring children to work together toward a common goal and by supporting their efforts in doing so. Readers theatre is not a competitive activity, but rather a cooperative one in which children share, discuss, and band together for the good of the production.

- It is valuable for non-English speaking children or non-fluent readers. It provides them with positive models of language usage and interpretation that extend far beyond the "decoding" of printed materials. It allows them to see "language in action" and the various ways in which language can be used.

- Teachers and librarians have discovered that readers theatre is an excellent way to enhance the development of communication skills. Voice projection, intonation, inflection, and pronunciation skills are all promoted within and throughout any readers theatre production. Children who need assistance in these areas are provided with a support structure that encourages the development of necessary abilities.

- It facilitates the development and enhancement of self concept. Because children are working in concert with other children in a supportive atmosphere, their self-esteem mushrooms. Again, the emphasis is on the presentation, not necessarily the performers. As such, students have opportunities to develop levels of self-confidence and self-assurance that would not normally be available in more traditional class productions.

- It enhances creative and critical thinking. Because children are active participants in the interpretation and delivery of a story, they develop thinking skills that are divergent rather than convergent and interpretive skills that are supported rather than directed.

- When children are provided with opportunities to write their own readers theatre script, their writing abilities are supported and encouraged. As children become familiar with the design and format of readers theatre scripts, they can begin to use their own creative talents in designing their own scripts and stories.

- It is fun! Children of all ages have delighted in using readers theatre for many years. It is delightful and stimulating, encouraging and fascinating, relevant and personal. Indeed, try as I might, I have not been able to locate a single instance (or group of students) in which (or for whom) readers theatre would not be an appropriate learning activity. It is an activity filled with a cornucopia of possibilities and promises.

Presentation Suggestions

It is important to remember that there is no single way to present readers theatre. What follows are some ideas you and the students with whom you work may wish to keep in mind as you put on the productions in this book. Different classes and even different groups of students within the same class will have their own methods and modes of presentation; in other words, it is possible that no two presentations will ever be the same. However, here are some suggestions that will help make any readers theatre performance successful.

Preparing Scripts

One of the advantages of using readers theatre in the classroom is the lack of extra work or preparation time necessary to get "up and running." By using the scripts in this book, your preparation time is minimal.

- After a script has been selected for presentation make sufficient copies. A copy of the script should be provided for each actor. In addition, two or three extra copies (one for you and replacement copies for scripts that are accidentally damaged or lost) is also a good idea. Copies for the audience are unnecessary and are not suggested.

- Each script can be bound between two sheets of colored construction paper or poster board. Bound scripts tend to formalize the presentation a little and lend an air of professionalism to the actors.

- Highlight each character's speaking parts with different color highlighter pens. This helps students track their parts without being distracted by the dialogue of others.

Starting Out

Introducing the concept of readers theatre to your students for the first time may be as simple as sharing a script with the entire class and walking them through the design and delivery of that script.

- Emphasize that a readers theatre performance does not require any memorization of the script. It's the interpretation and performance that count.

- You may wish to read through an entire script aloud taking on the various roles. Let students know how easy and comfortable this process is.

- Encourage selected volunteers to read assigned parts of a sample script to the entire class. Readers should stand or sit in a circle so that other classmates can observe them.

- Provide opportunities for additional re-readings using other volunteers. Plan time to discuss the ease of presentation and the different interpretations offered by different readers.

- Readers should have an opportunity to practice the script before presenting it to an audience. Take some time to discuss vocal intonation, facial gestures, body movements, and other features that could be used to enhance the presentation.

- Allow students the opportunity to suggest their own modifications, adaptations, or interpretations of the script. They will undoubtedly be attuned to the interests and perceptions of their peers and can offer some distinctive and personal interpretations.

- Encourage students to select non-stereotypical roles within any readers theatre script. For example, boys can take on female roles and girls can take on male roles, the smallest person in the class can take on the role of a giant, a shy student can take on the role of a boastful, bragging character. Provide sufficient opportunities for students to expand and extend their appreciation of readers theatre through a variety of "out of character" roles.

Staging

Staging involves the physical location of the readers as well as any necessary movements. Unlike a more formal play, the movements are minimal. The emphasis is more on presentation; less on action.

- For most presentations, readers will stand and/or sit on stools or chairs. The physical location of each reader has been indicated for the scripts in this book.

- The position of each reader is determined by "power of character" (Dixon, et al., 1996). This means that the main character is downstage center (in the middle front of the staging area), and the lesser characters are stage right, stage left, or further upstage (toward the rear of the staging area).

- If there are many characters in the presentation, it may be advantageous to have characters in the rear (upstage) standing while those in the front (downstage) are placed on stools or chairs. This ensures that the audience will both see and hear each actor.

- Usually all of the characters will be on stage throughout the entire presentation. For most presentations, it is not necessary to have characters enter and exit. If you place the characters on stools, they can face the audience when they are involved in a particular scene and then turn around whenever they are not involved in a scene.

- You may wish to make simple, hand-lettered signs with the name of each character. Loop a piece of string or yarn through each sign and hang it around the neck of each respective character. That way, the audience will know the identity of each character throughout the presentation.

- Slightly more formal presentations will have various characters entering and exiting at various times throughout the presentation. These directions are indicated in the scripts in this book.

- Each reader will have her or his own copy of the script in a paper cover (see above). If possible, use a music stand for each reader's script (this allows readers to use their hands for dramatic interpretations, as necessary).

- Several presentations have a narrator to set up the story. The narrator serves to establish the place and time of the story for the audience. Typically, the narrator is separated from the other actors and can be identified by a simple sign.

- As students become more comfortable with readers theatre invite them to suggest alternative positions for characters in a script. The placements indicated in these scripts are only suggestions; students may want to experiment with various staging possibilities. This becomes a worthwhile cooperative activity and demonstrates the variety of interpretations possible with any single script.

Props

Two of the positive features of readers theatre are the ease of preparation and the ease of presentation. Informality is a hallmark of any readers theatre script.

- Much of the setting for a story should take place in the audience's mind. Elaborate scenery is not necessary—simple props are often the best. For example:

  - A branch or potted plant can serve as a tree.

  - A drawing on the chalkboard can illustrate a building.

  - A hand-lettered sign can designate one part of the staging area as a particular scene (e.g., swamp, castle, field, forest).

  - Children's toys can be used for uncomplicated props (e.g., telephone, vehicles, etc.).

  - A sheet of aluminum foil or a remnant of blue cloth can be used to simulate a lake or pond.

- Costumes for the actors are unnecessary. Students may suggest a few simple items. For example:

  - Hats, scarves, or aprons can be used by major characters.

  - A paper cutout can serve as a tie, button, or badge.

  - Old clothing (borrowed from parents) can be used as warranted.

- Some teachers and librarians have discovered that the addition of appropriate music or sound effects can enhance a readers theatre presentation. For example, background music from the movie *2001* for a play about space exploration; the sound of rock and roll music in the background of a script about the 1960s; or the ticking of a clock in a story about futuristic events.

- It's important to remember that the emphasis in readers theatre is on the reading, not on any accompanying "features." The best presentations are often the simplest.

Delivery

I have often found it advantageous to let students know that the only difference between a readers theatre presentation and a movie role is the fact that they will have a script in their hands. This allows them to focus more on *presenting* a script rather than *memorizing* a script.

- When first introduced to readers theatre, students often tend to read "into" their scripts. Encourage students to look up from their scripts and interact with other characters or the audience, as necessary.

- Practicing the script beforehand can eliminate the problem of students burying their heads in the pages. In so doing, children understand the need to involve the audience as much as possible in the development of the story.

- Voice projection and delivery are important in order for the audience to understand character actions. The proper mood and intent need to be established, aspects which are possible when children are familiar and comfortable with each character's style.

- Children should *not* memorize their lines, but rather should rehearse them sufficiently so that they are comfortable with them. Again, the emphasis is on delivery, so be sure to suggest different types of voice that children may wish to use for their characters (e.g., angry, irritated, calm, frustrated, excited, etc.).

Post-Presentation

As a wise author once said, "The play's the thing." So it is with readers theatre. In other words, the mere act of presenting a readers theatre script is complete in and of itself. It is not necessary, or even required, to do any type of formalized evaluation after readers theatre. Once again, the emphasis is on informality. Readers theatre should and can be a pleasurable and stimulating experience for students.

What follows are a few ideas you may want to share with students. In doing so, you will be providing important languaging opportunities that extend and promote all aspects of your language arts program.

- After a presentation, discuss with students how the script enhanced or altered the original story.

- Invite students to suggest other characters who could be added to the script.

- Invite students to suggest new or alternate dialogue for various characters.

- Invite students to suggest new or different settings for the script.

- Invite students to talk about their reactions to various characters' expressions, tone of voice, presentations, or dialogues.

- After a presentation, invite youngsters to suggest any modifications or changes needed in the script.

- Invite each of the "cast" members to maintain a "production log" or reading response log in which they record their thoughts and perceptions about the presentation. Encourage them to share their logs with other class members.

Presenting a readers theatre script need not be an elaborate or extensive production. As students become more familiar and polished in using readers theatre, they will be able to suggest a multitude of presentation possibilities for future scripts. It is important to help students assume a measure of self-initiated responsibility in the delivery of any readers theatre. In so doing, you will be helping to ensure their personal engagement and active participation in this valuable language arts activity.

It is hoped that you and your students will find an abundance of readers theatre scripts in this book for use in your own classroom, but these scripts should also serve as an impetus for creating your own classroom or library scripts. By providing opportunities for your students to begin designing their own readers theatre scripts, you will be offering them an exciting new arena for enhancing their appreciation of science fiction and their role in its recreation.

References

Barchers, Suzanne. *Readers Theatre for Beginning Readers*. Englewood, CO: Teacher Ideas Press, 1993.

Dixon, Neill, Anne Davies, and Colleen Politano. *Learning with Readers Theatre: Building Connections*. Winnipeg, Canada: Peguis Publishers, 1996.

Fredericks, Anthony D. *Frantic Frogs and Other Frankly Fractured Folktales for Readers Theatre*. Englewood, CO: Teacher Ideas Press, 1993.

———. *Readers Theatre for American History*. Englewood, CO: Teacher Ideas Press, 2001.

———. *Silly Salamanders and Other Slightly Stupid Stories for Readers Theatre*. Englewood, CO: Teacher Ideas Press, 2000.

———. *Tadpole Tales and Other Totally Terrific Treats for Readers Theatre*. Englewood, CO: Teacher Ideas Press, 1997.

PART I

Distant Worlds, Distant Planets

Introduction

This script is a minute-by-minute account of the first landing by Martians on the planet Earth. It parallels events surrounding the first manned exploration of the Moon in 1969.

Staging

All the characters are news reporters. They can be seated facing the audience on chairs or stools. Each should be behind a desk, table, or music stand. If possible, place a fake microphone (made from construction paper) in front of each reporter. The narrator should be offstage and out of sight of the audience. The offstage voice also should be unseen.

Narrator

Reporter 1   Reporter 2   Reporter 3
X   X   X

Offstage Voice

NARRATOR: Exploring space has always held a special fascination. Distant planets and distant worlds offer an amazing array of discoveries. Many of the explorations have been conducted using highly sophisticated technology to send probes throughout the universe. The results have been phenomenal and exciting. New discoveries have been made and continue to be made all the time.

There are those, however, who have always questioned the need for space exploration and have been particularly concerned about the risks of sending individuals out into a dangerous and unfamiliar frontier. There always have been risks—but also the possibilities of incredible discoveries about worlds far removed from our own.

     The date is the present. There are clear skies over the launch site as the spacecraft is poised on the launch pad for one of the most historic flights in history.

Pause.

NARRATOR: Time: 9:32 A.M.

REPORTER 1:   The spacecraft is poised on the launch pad. Its crew is about to begin one of the most significant voyages of all time.

REPORTER 2:   This is a history-making voyage. The crew will travel to a planet never explored before, except through the use of telescopes, robots, and other mechanical aids.

REPORTER 3:   Look, the spacecraft is taking off. What an exciting time!

REPORTER 1:   The spacecraft has just left the launch pad. In 11 minutes it will reach an altitude of more than 120 miles and a speed of 17,400 miles per hour.

REPORTER 2:   Soon afterward, the first two stages of the spacecraft will drop away and fall to the surface.

REPORTER 3:   In less than three hours, the third stage will ignite and propel the spacecraft on a direct course toward the nearest planet—a planet of mystery, a planet of discovery.

NARRATOR: Time: 12:49 P.M.

REPORTER 1:   The spacecraft is traveling at a speed of 24,300 miles per hour.

REPORTER 2:   Now the crew must perform the first of several critical maneuvers. They must separate the landing vehicle from the rest of the spacecraft and reverse position in order to dock head-to-head with the command module still inside the spacecraft. *(Long pause.)* They did it! They are now separated from the third stage of the rocket and are on their way.

NARRATOR:	Time: 12:58 P.M.—three days after the launch.
REPORTER 3:	The spacecraft is closing in on the planet. The three astronauts have been monitoring their spacecraft making sure everything is in complete working order.
REPORTER 1:	Two hundred miles above the surface of the planet, the captain is giving the order to fire the rockets, so the spacecraft will slow to a speed of 3,600 miles per hour.
REPORTER 2:	The spacecraft has been captured by the planet's gravity and is entering an orbit 60 miles above the surface.
NARRATOR:	Time: 1:46 P.M.
REPORTER 3:	After 14 orbits around the planet, the spacecraft, with two astronauts, has separated from the command module.
NARRATOR:	Time: 3:08 P.M.
REPORTER 1:	The spacecraft's landing gear has just been released. They are descending to the surface of the planet.
REPORTER 2:	The spacecraft is now making a burn that drops it to within 50,000 feet of the planet's surface. The captain is looking out the window and carefully monitoring the landmarks below.
NARRATOR:	Time: 4:05 P.M.
REPORTER 3:	A second burn has begun that is positioning the spacecraft away from the planet's surface.
NARRATOR:	Time: 4:08 P.M.
REPORTER 1:	The captain is repositioning the spacecraft into a face-up position. The captain and the copilot are now flying with their backs to the surface.

NARRATOR:	Time: 4:10 P.M.
REPORTER 2:	*(Excitedly)* The spacecraft is at 6,000 feet. Wait! Two warning lights have just turned on. Wait! Okay, okay, Mission Control has given the go-ahead to ignore the lights. The mission can continue.
NARRATOR:	Time: 4:13 P.M.
REPORTER 3:	The on-board computer has moved the spacecraft into an upright position. The captain can clearly see the intended landing site. It's a large field with white lines running parallel to each other. The spacecraft has just enough fuel for five more minutes of flight.
NARRATOR:	Time: 4:15 P.M.
REPORTER 1:	The captain has decided to abandon the original landing site.
NARRATOR:	Time: 4:17 P.M.
REPORTER 2:	The captain has switched to manual control and has now flown over the field with white lines. He is slowing his rate of descent from approximately 20 feet per second to 3 feet per second.
NARRATOR:	Time: 4:18 P.M.
REPORTER 3:	The captain is 1,100 feet west of the white-lined field and is descending to a new landing spot.
REPORTER 1:	Now they're at 100 feet.
REPORTER 2:	75 feet.
REPORTER 3:	50 feet.
NARRATOR:	Time: 4:19 P.M.
REPORTER 1:	25 feet.

REPORTER 2:	15 feet.
REPORTER 3:	10 feet.
REPORTER 1:	5 feet.
OFFSTAGE VOICE:	The spacecraft has landed.
NARRATOR:	Time: 4:24 P.M.
REPORTER 2:	The captain is crawling out of the spacecraft feet first. He is descending the ladder.
REPORTER 3:	The captain has jumped down to the footpad, just a couple of inches from the surface.
REPORTER 1:	The captain is stepping out onto the surface!
OFFSTAGE VOICE:	That's one small step for a Martian, one giant leap for the citizens of Mars.
REPORTER 2:	History has been made.
REPORTER 3:	Martians have finally landed on the surface of the Earth.

Possible Extensions

1. Invite students to discuss the significance of space exploration. What have we learned about the universe since we began exploring space?

2. Encourage students to imagine that they have landed on the surface of a distant planet and have approximately 24 hours to spend any way they wish. What would they want to discover? What experiments would they want to do? What would they want to see?

3. Invite students to form two groups—one that supports the further exploration of space and one that argues against any further funding of space missions. Encourage students to discuss the funding of space missions versus the funding for social problems here at home. Which is more critical? Which is more important?

Introduction

Scientists on a distant planet are on the verge of discovering an ancient and unusual artifact. Nobody can figure out what it is, which makes it even more interesting.

Staging

The staging area is set up to resemble an archeological site. Two workers (1 and 2) are in the background simulating digging and other exploring activities. Additional "archeologists" are positioned around the staging area and are engaged in simulated activities at an examining table or with microscopes. Characters can exit and enter randomly to convey an atmosphere of activity.

Worker 1   Worker 2
X   X

Worker 3   Worker 4
X   X

Dr. Diggs   Reporter   Worker 5
X   X   X

Narrator
X

NARRATOR: The setting is in the future. A special team of skilled archeologists has been dispatched to the surface of the planet Mercury. Highly sensitive space probes, launched nearly a year ago, detected an unusual object just below the surface of the planet. Scientists aren't sure what it is, but they are eager to find out. Excitement is in the air as one reporter is assigned to the team to bring back a first-hand account of this potentially exciting discovery. For the first time, an interview from a distant planet is being broadcast to the people of Earth.

REPORTER: Tell me, Dr. Diggs, what do you hope to accomplish on this archeological excavation?

DR. DIGGS: We hope to find out exactly what the Spiros III space probe located beneath the surface of the planet. It is not something we were able to recognize on the computer screen, and we need to find out what it was.

WORKER 1:   *(Running)* Dr. Diggs, Dr. Diggs, we've just broken through the permafrost and are within reach of the object.

DR. DIGGS: Good. Make sure the area is sealed off. I don't want any type of contamination. *(The worker returns to his post.)*

REPORTER: This is very exciting. There's a lot of activity taking place here. Is it always this way at a dig?

DR. DIGGS: Yes. Usually there are many more archeologists on a site, but, as you know, funding for distant planet archeological recovery projects has been severely limited in recent years. Thus, we were only able to bring a skeleton crew on this expedition.

REPORTER: Do you have any idea what you're looking for?

DR. DIGGS: No, and we think that's the most exciting part of a Distant Planet dig. Humans have been on their planet for only a brief period of time—at least in relation to the age of the universe. What we don't know is whether or not other bodies in space have ever been visited by superior beings from inside or outside our own universe.

WORKER 3:   *(Excitedly)* Professor, we're showing an object about six meters below the surface. It's cylindrical in shape and appears to have a bright yellow color.

DR. DIGGS:	Well, let me know when you get within a meter of it. It could be contaminated, and we want to be sure that the crew is not exposed to it without the necessary protection. *(The worker exits.)*
REPORTER:	Now, this is getting exciting! By the way, *(pointing to Worker 4 and Worker 5)* what are those two scientists doing?
DR. DIGGS:	They're setting up scientific instruments designed to analyze the composition of the soil surrounding the object. We need to be sure that we don't disturb the area around this object unnecessarily and that we don't release any toxic materials into the atmosphere.
REPORTER:	*(Walking over to Worker 4 and Worker 5)* Can you two tell our viewing audience what you are doing?
WORKER 4:	Sure, we're implanting a bio-analyzer just under the surface. This instrument is able to accurately analyze the composition of the surrounding soil and compare it to all the known soils in the solar system. That way, we'll be able to tell if this planet is in any way related to other planets that may have been created at the same time.
WORKER 5:	What's important here is that we retrieve whatever object is below the surface and also that we take samplings of the surrounding area. That way, if we ever encounter this type of soil on another planet or in another solar system, we'll have a better idea of what we are looking at.
REPORTER:	This all seems so complicated. I just thought you were going to look for the strange object seen by the probe, pack it up, and take it back to Earth for months of scientific analysis.
WORKER 4:	Well, actually most of our scientific work is done in the field, not in a laboratory. Sure, whatever object is lying below the surface is important, but we must take stock of the surrounding area so that we can put everything into its proper context.

WORKER 1: *(Excitedly running up to Dr. Diggs)* Professor, Professor! We are within five centimeters of the object. We should know what it is in a few minutes.

Everyone gathers around in the back of the staging area. They all peer into the center of the dig that Worker 1 and Worker 2 have been working on.

REPORTER: This is exciting! For the first time in the history of space exploration we are able to report on an archeological dig that may reveal the origins of the universe.

WORKER 3: We're just breaking through. The instruments are spinning around like crazy!

WORKER 5: *(Excitedly)* Look, there it is! What is it? I've never seen one of these before.

WORKER 4: Dr. Diggs, what is that?

DR. DIGGS: *(Peering into the hole)* I'm not sure. This is not what we expected. There's no explanation for it.

WORKER 2: *(Reaching into the hole)* Wow! Does anyone have any idea what this is?

WORKER 1: It looks like a tool from an ancient civilization. But, how would it ever be used? It looks completely useless. It doesn't make any sense!

Worker 2 holds up a yellow, number two pencil. Everyone stares at it in amazement.

REPORTER: This is truly a mystery, folks. It looks like months of scientific analysis will be needed before this object and its uses can be identified. But, it's obvious to this reporter that the civilization that produced this object was unsophisticated and backward. Surely, they died out many, many centuries ago. Perhaps, we'll never know.

Possible Extensions

1. Invite an archeologist from a local college or university to speak to students about some of the procedures and practices used on archeological digs. Students may wish to investigate the training and education necessary to become an archeologist.

2. Invite students to create their own readers theatre scripts centering on a recent archeological find (e.g., discovery of new dinosaur fossils).

3. Invite students to create a fictitious travel brochure about the planet Mercury. What are some of the most interesting sites? Where are they located? What are some activities that can be done on the planet?

Introduction

A group of colonists is about to land on the planet Jupiter. Before they do, they must establish a form of government to ensure the survival of this new colony. Their discussions parallel those that took place prior to the landing of the *Mayflower* at Plymouth Rock.

Staging

The characters can be seated on stools or chairs around a large table or desk. The narrators should be standing off to each side of the staging area.

```
                          Tor
                           X
        ┌──────────────────────────────────────┐
Marra   │                                      │   Cray
  X     │                                      │     X
        │                                      │
        │                                      │
Senn    │                                      │   Krile
  X     │                                      │     X
        │                                      │
        │                                      │
Rak     │                                      │   Bli
  X     └──────────────────────────────────────┘     X


     Narrator 1                              Narrator 2
         X                                       X
```

15

NARRATOR 1:   The year is 2384. A group of 7,149 men and women have boarded an old space ferry named *The Intrepid* and set off for the planet Jupiter. Many of these people own stock in The Intergalactic Company, a company that hopes to establish itself on a new planet. A small group of individuals (later known as The Chosen) on board the spaceship are leaving the planet Mars to seek peace on another planet.

NARRATOR 2:   For centuries, the colonies on the planet Mars have been engaged in a brutal and destructive war. Each colony wants ever-larger pieces of territory. Colonies survive (or die) based on their ability to find rockinite—a precious metal discovered many centuries earlier by the first settlers from the planet Earth. Rockinite was used as a prime source of power for the colonies that sprang up across the Martian landscape. Unfortunately, there was a limited supply of the precious metal. Colonies began to battle with each other to claim more land and thus more rockinite. The Great Wars raged on, century after century. Now finally, only three colonies are left, and one of those colonies—Alpha Major IV— has decided to leave the turmoil on Mars and set out in search of a new planet upon which they can build a peaceful society.

NARRATOR 1:   As *The Intrepid* heads for Jupiter, a fierce Jovian storm drives the spaceship to the northern pole of the planet. As they hover above the surface Tor, the leader of the group, wants to make sure that all the colonists work together for the good of the colony. He presents an agreement for the colonists to consider.

Scene One

TOR: Greetings to all. Before we set foot on this new planet below us, I want to present a document to this body. This document has been prepared as a pact—an agreement among all those who gather here and are on board this spaceship. This pact is for preserving our freedoms, for ensuring our liberties, and for establishing civil guarantees.

KRILE: *(Angry and pounding his fist on the table)* Hey, just who do you think you are? What makes you think you can just create some document that tells us what we can and cannot do? You must think this is going to be some kind of dictatorship, right?

CRAY: *(In a calming voice)* Hey, Krile, old buddy, just settle down. All we're trying to do is establish a colony that works. We don't want any of the trouble we left behind on Mars.

TOR: That's right. We propose a government that is set by the people. This government shall be one of free rights. We shall be able to set laws that are for the basic good of everyone.

KRILE: *(Still angry)* Laws, shmaws! This is all just a bunch of junk if you ask me. You're trying to imprison us before we even get set up on this new planet.

SENN: *(Upset)* Yeah, my buddy Krile here knows what he's talking about. Why do we need this pact anyway? It's just a way of keeping the colonists under the thumb of some government people. If you ask me, this is all a bunch of junk!

TOR: *(Soothingly)* Hey, just calm down now. All we're trying to do is provide some kind of internal protection—a set of laws and rules that will help us get along and survive in an alien world.

BLI: *(Angrily)* Hey, I'm with these guys. Look, Mr. Tor, I don't know who put you in power here, but all of us have just traveled over a couple zillion miles of space and we're not about to throw it all away by some set of laws or rules or regulations or whatever you want to call them just to turn this new colony into some sort of dictatorship. It sounds to me like you want all the power just because you're the captain of this ship.

RAK: *(Threateningly)* I say Mr. Tor here is just trying to be King Tor—King Tor of the Planet Jupiter. *(Pounding the table)* I say we throw out his little pact and run the colony the way *we* want to run the colony . . . not *his* way!

EVERYONE: *(Loudly)* Yeah! Yeah! Yeah!

The people around the table are all yelling and arguing with Tor, and then the conversation slowly fades away.

Scene Two

Tor is absent from the table

NARRATOR 1:   *The Intrepid* has landed on the surface of Jupiter. Tor has been exiled from the ship and must face the elements of outer space on his own. He is destined to die a slow and painful death.

NARRATOR 2:   Meanwhile, back aboard the ship, the colonists are, once again, seated around the table. There is much disagreement and arguing. It looks as though the new colony is doomed before it even begins.

BLI: *(Frustrated)* I don't get it. Can't we just all agree on some form of government? Why does there have to be all this arguing?

RAK: *(To everyone)* I've had it with you guys. All you do is argue and argue. Nobody can agree on anything. I've just had it! *(Gets up and leaves)*

KRILE: *(Angrily)* Look, we're getting nowhere fast. If we don't make a decision soon about how we are going to govern or what laws we are going to have, then we're going to wind up killing one another and there won't be any colony at all. This whole journey will have been for nothing!

MARRA: I hate to admit it, but Krile is right! If we don't do something soon we're going to wind up fighting each other. After that . . . no colony!

SENN: *(In a calm voice)* I think Krile and Marra have given us something to think about. But, what do we do now?

Everyone gets up from the table and slowly walks offstage. They all look confused. After a minute they slowly return and sit down at the table again.

Scene Three

The characters are quietly talking to each other in pairs.

NARRATOR 1: The atmosphere around the table is considerably calmer now. The colonists have come to the conclusion that if they don't work together, they may all perish together.

NARRATOR 2: A piece of paper has been brought to the table. Members of the group are pointing to and discussing this document.

BLI: *(Pointing to the document)* So, where did you find this thing?

SENN: It was part of an old history book I found in the library area of the ship. I think the book was one used in school by our great great grandparents or something like that. Anyway, as you can see, it's very old.

CRAY: So, what does this old piece of paper say? Does it have any answers for our situation?

KRILE: I sure hope so. Because if we don't find any answers soon . . . well . . .

MARRA: Well, let's listen to what Senn has to say. *(To Senn)* Why don't you go ahead and tell us what the name of this paper is that you discovered.

SENN: Okay. It says here at the top that this is "The Constitution of the United States of America."

NARRATOR 1: After much discussion, and with a few modifications, the colonists decided to accept the document. In later years, this document became the standard for a form of government in all the colonies.

NARRATOR 2: In late 2384, the colonists began building a small settlement near the northern ice cap of Jupiter. For nearly seven centuries this small, independent settlement on Jupiter survived under their rule of self-government. It wasn't until the Tremarian Invasion that the colony was to find out just how strong their government was.

Possible Extensions

1. Invite students to create a "Constitution" for the classroom. Encourage them to imagine that their class is the first colony on a new planet. What guarantees, rights, and privileges would they want in their new colony?

2. Invite students to discuss what the term "self-government" means to them. How might that concept differ from other forms of government? What are some of its advantages? What are some of its challenges?

3. Invite students to create their own readers theatre script about the first 10 years of the new colony on Jupiter. What happens to them? What happens to the colonies they left behind on the planet Mars?

4. Invite students to create a script about the Tremarian Invasion. How does the Jovian Pact help the colonists survive this great conflict?

Introduction

A group of travelers is journeying across the New Frontier. There are adventures waiting them—along with the possibility of creatures and troglodytes. It's a frightening time in an unknown land.

Staging

The narrator can be placed on a podium or at lectern near the front of the staging area. The characters should be seated on stools or chairs arranged in two rows of three chairs each (to simulate the positions they might have in a forward-moving vehicle). The characters are all facing the direction of the arrow.

```
    Mr. Samuels        Todd            Cara
        X                X               X


<--------


    Mrs. Samuels       Matt            Cass
        X                X               X


  Narrator 1                       Narrator 2
      X                                 X
```

NARRATOR 1:   It is an exciting time—brave adventurers seeking a better life, seeking new lands to explore and settle, are crossing the New Frontier. The dangers are many, but the prospects of wide-open spaces and a new way of life draw thousands of travelers to seek their fortunes.

21

NARRATOR 2: This is the great unknown; few stories have come back to the adventurers about the land they are about to cross. There are rumors about troglodytes who attack the long lines of travelers—killing many and destroying property. But these are stories that have been told many times and cannot always be counted as fact. They are frightening nevertheless, for they underscore the dangers that may be ahead and the unknowns the travelers must face in a hostile environment.

NARRATOR 1: It is the fourth year of the crossing. Seven groups of travelers have made the journey, and although nobody is sure about the fate of those first travelers, there is hope, determination, and optimism that this group will make it safely across the New Frontier. They are setting out for a new life and new possibilities. Let's look in at one family.

TODD: Hey, how long did you say this trip across the New Frontier was going to take us?

MR. SAMUELS: According to our leader, this trip should take us from four to six months.

CASS: That's a long time. How come it takes so long?

MR. SAMUELS: We're traveling a great distance, Cass. It's a big, wide territory that we have to get across.

MATT: Hey, look over there. *(Pointing)* See? There's a big group of critters standing over there. Wow. I've never seen so many before.

CASS: Yes, look at them. There's more here than we ever saw back home. I guess this territory is full of surprises.

MRS. SAMUELS: It sure is. Remember the strange creatures we saw the other day? I can't recall seeing that many in one place before. There must have been at least a thousand of them standing around and staring at us.

MATT: *(Excitedly)* Yeah, that sure was a strange sight!

MR. SAMUELS:	I suspect that we're going to see lots of strange sights on this journey.
CARA:	What else do you suppose we'll see?
MR. SAMUELS:	We'll probably see those geologic formations everyone's been talking about.
TODD:	Hey, are those geologic formations as tall as everyone says they are? I mean, do they really reach up into the sky?
MR. SAMUELS:	That's what I hear. I also hear that it's going to take a lot of work by everyone to get across them.
CASS:	How are we going to get across? Do you think we're going to have to climb them by ourselves?
MRS. SAMUELS:	We'll make it across with a lot of hard work and determination. We all knew this was going to be a tough journey and that we might face difficult obstacles.
TODD:	I'm just worried about the Great Cold setting in. I know it's going to be hard getting across the geologic formations, but it's going to be even more difficult if we don't get across before the Great Cold. We would never make it.
MATT:	You know what? I'm a little scared of the troglodytes. We've never seen troglodytes before, and I'm afraid of what they might do.
MRS. SAMUELS:	Now, don't worry about it. Remember after we saw the strange creatures a while back, we also saw some troglodytes off in the distance? They didn't do anything. They just sat and watched us. I think they were more interested in the strange creatures than they were in us.
MATT:	Maybe you're right. But I'm still afraid of them.
CARA:	So am I.
CASS:	After we get across the geologic features, what happens next?

MR. SAMUELS: Well, according to our leader, we come to the Distant Land. We'll go on down to our new home. We'll go on down to the beautiful New Territory.

TODD: Where do you think we'll live?

MR. SAMUELS: We don't know yet. We haven't decided that yet. But I do know it will be very different from where we used to live.

CASS: Will we live by the Great Sea? Can we live by the Great Sea?

MR. SAMUELS: We'll have to wait. We'll take a look around and just see what we see. I don't know yet, but we'll find a place the whole family will like.

MRS. SAMUELS: It will be beautiful, children. We know that. It will be beautiful, and we will be able to build our new house and build our new life in the New Territory. It sure is exciting.

MR. SAMUELS: Yes, it sure is exciting.

MATT: I can hardly wait.

NARRATOR 2:   The people who crossed the New Frontier faced a lot of hardships. Troglodytes sometimes attacked, trying to prevent the settlers from moving across the land. There were dangerous conditions in the geologic formations.

NARRATOR 1:   Transportation was unreliable and required frequent repairs. The vehicles moved across the land on cushions of air—an ancient form of propulsion. The generators often broke down and the settlers would have to repair them. Each vehicle was only 5,000 square feet and could accommodate only a single family and a few of its possessions. But, the settlers endured.

NARRATOR 2:   In spite of all the hardships, people continued to cross the New Frontier. By 2278 there were more than 5,000 settlers living in the New Territory. It was truly an exciting time on Io, one of the 16 moons of Jupiter.

Possible Extensions

1. Invite students to make a list of materials and supplies that the settlers in this story would have needed for their survival. How does that list compare with a list that might have been made by the Pilgrims in the early 1600s?

2. Encourage students to create a readers theatre sequel to the script above. What adventures would the Samuels have experienced in their new home? What did they discover about the New Territory that they didn't know before their journey?

3. Invite students to plot a journey of 2,000 miles across the continental U.S. What supplies would they take with them? What form of transportation would they use? How would their journey be different from a journey across the New Frontier? How would it be similar?

NOTE: This script can be used as an effective follow-up to "Artifact." The two scripts together can become part of a larger unit on archeology—a way to blend science, science fiction, and social studies into an engaging and dynamic unit of study. Each of the two scripts can also be used as a stand-alone script—one near the beginning of a science fiction unit, the other near the end of the unit.

Set-up

Before this script can be performed, you will need to create several "artifacts" (see below). These artifacts will provide students (the actors as well as the audience) with opportunities to engage in some scientific speculating and predicting. Have these artifacts ready prior to the performance.

Materials

Several cups of playground sand (Large, 50-pound bags can be purchased at most hardware stores. Smaller bags can be obtained at a pet store or an aquarium supply store.)

Several large containers of white glue, such as Elmer's Glue®

Large mixing bowl

Tablespoon

Cookie sheet

Several coins (see below)

Nonstick cooking spray

Large jar (a mayonnaise or pickle jar works well)

Water

Oven

Directions

1. Place 2 cups of playground sand into a large mixing bowl.

2. Add 2 cups of white glue.

3. Mix the sand and glue together until it is the consistency of wet cement. (You may wish to adjust the measurements.)

4. Drop by tablespoonfuls onto a cookie sheet that has been sprayed with a nonstick coating, such as Pam®. Use the same procedure you would practice in making homemade cookies.

5. Into each "cookie" on the sheet, press a single coin (penny, nickel, dime, quarter).

6. Use your fingers to wrap the dough completely around each individual coin.

7. Place the cookie sheet into a warm oven (250 degrees), and bake for approximately 3 to 4 hours.

8. Remove the cookie sheet and allow the homemade rocks to cool for 24 hours. (Each "rock" will have the consistency of sandstone.)

9. Prior to the production, provide a selection of homemade rocks to the players.

Important Notes

1. The rocks should be prepared by an adult in advance of the production. However, the recipe is simple enough that students (under supervision) may wish to prepare the rocks on their own.

2. *Do not* bake the rocks in a microwave oven.

3. Instead of using a conventional oven, place a sheet of the prepared rocks (wet) in a sunny location. Allow them to dry in the sun for 2 to 3 days to get the same results.

Production Note

This script is open-ended. It allows for participation by the audience, and it has no single conclusion. It does, however, provide you with an opportunity to demonstrate a portion of scientific procedure (hypothesis, experiment, conclusion). Different groups of students will arrive at different conclusions. You may wish to use this script as a prelude to an examination of the scientific procedures and practices used by all working scientists.

Staging

The characters are all standing around a table set up in the middle of the staging area. Several "rocks" have been placed on the table. Also on the table is the jar which has been filled one-third full with water.

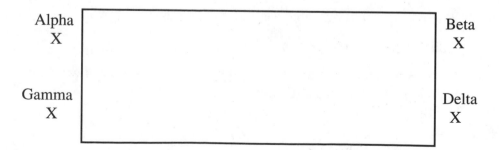

ALPHA:

Well, my fellow scientists, this has truly been a most successful mission.

BETA:

You are right. Our intrepid explorers have journeyed to the mysterious planet at the far end of the galaxy and have been able to retrieve several samples.

GAMMA:

(Picking up one of the rocks) They have done well. You see, here we have artifacts. It is an excellent sample—one that we should be able to examine in great detail.

DELTA:

We should be proud of our explorers, for they overcame great obstacles and many dangers in order to gather these samples for analysis. For the first time in the history of this planet, we are able to learn something about a distant world—a distant planet that is, in many ways, quite similar to our own—at least according to some of our preliminary scientific missions.

ALPHA:

But this is the first time we have been able to gather actual samples from the surface of that planet. *(Picks up one of the rocks and studies it carefully.)* I hope that our tests will reveal something about the composition of it.

BETA:

(Picking up one of the rocks) Certainly we shall learn something about the composition of the soil—perhaps even something about how the planet originally came to be—its genesis so to speak.

GAMMA:

(Turning the rock over and over, studying it closely) This could be the breakthrough we have been hoping for, the breakthrough that will reveal the universe's greatest and most mysterious secret—is there life on other worlds?

DELTA:

Perhaps we should begin our initial experiment. *(Everyone nods.)*

Delta picks up three to five of the rocks from the surface of the table and places them inside the large jar. The lid is screwed onto the top of the jar. During the next segment of the script Delta continuously shakes the jar back and forth in order to agitate the contents.

The next portion of the production depends on the breakdown of the rocks inside the jar. As Delta shakes the jar back and forth the rocks will rub against each other and begin to break down (similar to the process of water erosion in nature). They will continue to break down until they are reduced to sand. The coins which were previously embedded in the rocks will be revealed. This breakdown process will take two to five minutes to complete. The actors might need to adjust the pace of the next section of the production according to the speed at which the rocks are reduced.

ALPHA: *(Looking intently at the jar)* I see you have filled the experimental container with the decomposing agent.

DELTA: Yes, I thought we would begin with this part of the experiment. I am predicting that the samples are quite similar to those which are prevalent in the great sandy regions of our own world.

BETA: I notice that you are only using a few of the samples. Do you have any plans for the other samples?

DELTA: Yes, but I thought it would be important for us to examine the composition first. It would be most interesting to know if there are any life forms—at least life forms that we might be familiar with—on this new world.

GAMMA: Do we have any other evidence that there may be life forms or some existence of organic materials on this new world.

ALPHA: No, we can only guess that because these samples are similar, in some respects, to what we have on our own planet they might, at least in theory, be from a planet that has some type of life form or used to have some type of life form.

BETA: *(Pointing to jar)* Look. There are some things that are being revealed from inside the samples. *(Everyone comes in closer and stares at the contents of the jar as Delta continues the agitation process.)*

GAMMA:	It appears that there are some circular objects inside the samples.
BETA:	You are right. As I see it, there are several different objects being revealed by the agitation process.
ALPHA:	Let's watch closely. I believe our colleague *(nods toward Delta)* may have given us some critical information.
GAMMA:	Yes, look *(points)* there inside the chamber! Look carefully. There is some type of printing, some symbols on each of the objects.

Delta stops the agitation process. The jar is opened and each of the scientists reaches into the jar and obtains one or more of the coins which were embedded in each of the rocks.

BETA:	Look. There are several inscriptions on the circular objects that were in the samples.
ALPHA:	Yes, I can see them, too.
DELTA:	There are some unusual ones on mine as well. Perhaps we should try to decipher these. Perhaps they will tell us something about the world from which they came. Perhaps they will tell us about life forms that may have been, at one time, inhabitants of that world.
ALPHA:	*(Picking up a penny and examining it closely)* As I look at this artifact I can see that there were rectangular structures on this world. These structures appeared to have columns in the front. *(Looking at the audience)* Hmm, I wonder what this information reveals about the ways in which these life forms lived.
BETA:	*(Picking up a nickel and examining it closely)* Looking at this artifact, I clearly can see a life form that has a long strand of material hanging from the back of its head. *(Looking at the audience)* Hmmm, I wonder what this information reveals about the appearance of the life forms on that planet.

GAMMA: *(Picking up a dime and examining it closely)* As I look at this particular artifact, I see a torch with a flame coming out of the top. *(Looking at the audience)* Hmmm, I wonder what this reveals about the ways in which the life forms on the planet provided light during their dark hours or perhaps how they might have prepared their foods.

DELTA: *(Picking up a quarter and examining it closely)* This, too, is a most unusual artifact. In looking at it closely I can see a large creature with enormous wings at its side. Perhaps this is some sort of idol which the life forms on this world celebrate or pray to. *(Looking at the audience)* Hmmm, I wonder what this information reveals about the customs or traditions of the life forms on that planet.

Possible Extension

1. At this point in the production, the audience can be divided into four separate groups. Each of the groups is led by one of the scientists in the production. Each scientist gives the members of his or her group the artifact that he or she was examining. The members of the group carefully study all the inscriptions, figures, letters, numbers, and illustrations on each coin. The groups are encouraged to arrive at some conclusions about the life forms that created these artifacts. (In short, if these were the only artifacts available to a group of scientists, what conclusions would they be able to draw about the life forms that created them?) It is suggested that students engage in some cross-group discussions regarding the information they have gathered from the coins. (This extension could be used as a prelude to a social studies or science lesson about artifacts gathered from an archeological dig and what they might reveal to scientists concerning the people who left them.)

PART II

Creatures, Real and Otherwise

A MATTER OF SURVIVAL

Introduction

A group of nomads is attempting to eke out an existence in a harsh and bitter land. Their life is difficult and their journey is not easy, but they endure.

Staging

The narrators sit on stools or chairs at the front of the staging area. The characters (who are designated by letters, rather than names) are seated on the floor in a circle.

```
              B           C
              X           X

         A                     D
         X                     X

                   E
                   X

Narrator 1                              Narrator 2
    X                                       X
```

NARRATOR 1: It is the present. A small group of nomads has been traveling for nearly 10 months. They have left their base and are crossing a great wilderness. They are weary. As we look in on this group, they are talking about the day's activities.

A: This was a good day. We have traveled far and have been very successful in finding food for our group. We will eat well for the next day.

B: Tell us of your hunt. What creatures did you see? Where did you go?

35

C: We walked the way of our ancestors, like this. *(Gets up, walks around the group, then sits down)* They, too, walked far in search of the creatures. According to legend, they were able to find many different kinds of creatures to kill to feed their people.

NARRATOR 2:   The group is following the migrations of many creatures. The paths they use are the same paths used by these creatures. Often these paths are hard and blackened. Many of the paths are streaked with white or yellow. The nomads know that as long as they follow the creatures, they will find sufficient food.

A: *(Gesturing)* Today we found several creatures. They move rapidly, so we had to be very careful. We discovered some sleeping creatures. Several of us walked quietly around them. The soft soles of our foot-huggers muffled any sounds that we made.

E: Were you scared?

C: No. There were many of us and few of them.

B: It has been a long time since we have seen the creatures. We have found a few small creatures running across a large grassy area, but a large creature would feed our clan for many weeks.

NARRATOR 1:   The creatures are important to the survival of the nomads. The wanderers use the creatures' skin for clothing and various coverings that help protect them from cold weather. Bones from the creatures are used as weapons. The meat from a single creature can feed a tribe of nomads for several days.

D: Tell us more.

C: *(Simulating the movements)* There were 10 of us, and we surrounded the creatures inside a small wooden structure. Quietly, we approached them. Fortunately, because of our size, the creatures could not detect us. At a signal from our leader we each threw a weapon at the creatures. They awoke and made loud noises. Some of them began to run directly at two of us.

E: And then what happened?

A: *(Simulating the movements)* Many of us began to run, but the creatures stumbled. Eight weapons found their mark and the creatures lost much fluid. They got weaker. We all stayed away from them until they fell down. As the creatures were dying, we approached cautiously. It was almost an hour before we felt safe enough to touch them.

E: And then what did you do?

C: We each took a sharp stone that we carry whenever we go on a hunt. We cut up the meat for cooking. Then we placed the meat on sticks and held it over the fires.

NARRATOR 2: These nomads' survival was entirely dependent on the creatures they hunted. If there was a dry, dusty expanse, then there were few creatures along the way. On the other hand, large gatherings of these creatures could be found at places where there were loud noises. But the loud noises disturbed the hunters, and they stayed away. Also, different types of creatures had varying migration patterns. Finding the creatures was often a matter of chance.

D: The creatures are good providers, but we cannot depend on them alone. We have had difficulty in the past finding gatherings of them. Shouldn't we look for other food sources, too?

A: Yes. Legends from those who have passed this way before tell of long periods of time when there were no creatures. These legends also tell of a time when our ancestors encountered great hardships and often perished in the wilderness.

B: We must be cautious, and we must plan wisely.

C: *(Excitedly)* The creatures move all the time. Many are in metal enclosures that travel across the land at great speeds. They, too, are looking for food to sustain them. Sometimes they will stop to obtain their food from large, rectangular structures covered with the colors of dying leaves. If we do not find the creatures we will die. If we kill too many of the creatures there will not be enough to provide for us in the future.

D: Our lives are not easy. We depend on the creatures we seek. They not only guide us, but they also provide for our needs.

A: It has been a long day, and we must prepare for tomorrow's hunt.

C: Our weapons are few, but they have helped us. The large bones and stones we use help us kill the creatures we need. It is time to gather our weapons together.

B: Tomorrow will be another long day. It will be a day of hunting, a day of searching, a day of surviving.

D: And we will survive—as our ancestors did and as our children and their children will after us.

NARRATOR 1:   The group of individuals you see behind me are part of the third wave of aliens originally from the high plains of Mars. It was only a few centuries ago when the first wave of Martians crash-landed on this blue planet. Their only form of transportation was completely demolished, and all forms of communication were also been destroyed. They were left with few tools and even fewer materials they could use to survive in this strange land.

NARRATOR 2:   For a long time these nomads have wandered in small bands seeking the food they need to sustain themselves and the shelter necessary to protect them from the elements. They hunt because hunting provides them with both food and shelter. Each day, they continue their journey across the landscape. And, if they are lucky, they will discover and kill one or more of the creatures upon which their survival depends. Eventually, they will learn to call these creatures by their given name—humans.

Possible Extensions

1. Invite students to create their own readers theatre script about the discovery of a new land or new planet by a "shipwrecked" group of explorers. What new discoveries would they make? What adventures would they face on the new planet or new territory?

2. Invite students to go back through this script to look for clues that might indicate specifically the type of creature described (before the Narrator tells the audience). For example, "Sometimes they will stop to obtain their food from large, rectangular structures covered with the colors of dying leaves." Does this indicate a very popular type of fast food restaurant (McDonald's®)?

3. Invite students to discuss any similarities between the individuals in this script and individuals who are thought to have crossed the Bering Strait approximately 12,000 years ago and who traveled into what is now North America.

ME, MYSELF, AND I

Introduction

This script is set in the future. Clones are more than just a possibility; they are a reality. As you might expect, there are some interesting conversations when you meet your clone.

Staging

There are three characters in this production. The second and third characters are clones of the first character. During selected parts of the script two (or three) characters will be speaking back and forth (completing each other's sentences). This may take a little practice. If possible, all three characters should be dressed identically (white t-shirts and jeans, for example). The narrator stands off to the side and is positioned behind a lectern or on a podium. The three characters address the audience.

Narrator
X

A   B   C
X   X   X

NARRATOR: In the last decade, medical science has made enormous advances. Diseases that once ravaged Earth have been eliminated, life spans have increased dramatically, and the general health of people around the world has improved significantly. But there is a small group of scientists working in a secret laboratory high in the Sierra Nevada Mountains who have stumbled on one of nature's greatest and most mysterious secrets. At first there were only a few, limited tests. Then, with each success, the tests grew bolder, and the scientists grew braver. Finally, on a dark and windy night in an underground laboratory, the scientists did what had never been done before—they cloned a human being.

A:

I am the original human being. For most of my life I lived in Los Angeles. I was married and had two children. We lived in a small house with our dog and cat. But one day, one horrible day, all of that came to an end. An evil man came into my house and killed my wife and children. Murdered them, right there in my own home. My entire family was wiped out. I lost everything—everything I had ever loved, everything I had ever cherished. I couldn't endure it. I began to hate every human being that ever lived, all the violence, all the horrible things that people do to each other. "Why," I shouted, "do people have to do terrible things to each other?" I couldn't answer my own question. I was angry, and I couldn't stand it anymore. I sold my possessions and moved up high into the mountains. I built a log cabin and lived off the land. I had no electricity, no computer, no TV, no anything. It was just me and the animals and large, wide open spaces. No people to bother me, no cell phones to disturb me. I didn't want to be around anything or anybody. It was a human who had killed my wife and children, and I just couldn't stand the thought of being near any other humans. I didn't want to be hurt.

The original human pauses before continuing with his tale.

Then one day, a stranger passed my way. He greeted me and asked me a question I will never forget. He asked, "Would you like some company?" At first, I thought he was asking me if he could stay in my cabin. But I soon learned, that was the furthest thing from his mind. He was actually asking me if I would like to have *myself* as company. At first I didn't understand, but the more he talked, the more I learned. The more I learned, the more interested I became.

I went with him to a place I had never seen before—a place I never knew about, high in the mountains. It was a place away from cities, away from civilization, and away from all the chaos down below. There I met others like the stranger, others who would change my life as it had never been changed before. For now I am two.

B: Because I am his clone.

A: I am not one person,

B: but rather I am two people.

A: We are the same as each other.

B: Each of us is an identical twin of the other.

A: Two people,

B: one person.

A: We are the same.

B: We are each other.

A: I know you might find this difficult to believe, but I am no longer lonely. I have myself as company. I guess you could say that I am my own best friend. In fact, I may be the greatest friend I've ever had. Right now I have no need for other people; other people are not necessary in my life. I thought I liked people, but that was a long time ago. Now, I just don't care about them. I don't like what they do to each other. I guess, in a way, I just like me best. I like me, and I live with me. Because, you see, the scientists have created clones of me. Yes, I've become my own best friend.

A: Now I am three.

B: I am a clone of myself

C: and of me.

A: I am not one.

B: I am not two.

C: I am three.

A: Each of us is the same as the others.

B: Each one is identical to the other two.

C: We are three people,

A: but we are one person.

B: We are clones,

C: and all of us are each other.

A: I like being with me. I am my very best friend. *(Pointing)* I know what they know and what they are thinking because what they are thinking is the same as what I am thinking. I know that seems difficult to understand simply because each of you, like I once was, is an individual person. But, I am no longer an individual. I am three—all the same, all identical, all equal. We know each other as well as we know ourselves. I may be three people,

B: but I am one person.

A: I like myself best.

B: I am never afraid of myself.

A: So I will never fear who I am or what I will do.

B: I do not do terrible things, so I know my clones will never hurt me like other people do because they are me.

A: I answer to me.

B: I live only with me, but I am never alone.

A: I live only with me but I am never lonely.

C: I live with them, but I live only with me.

B: You live with other people, and I don't,

C: but I am not alone.

A: That's the difference. Here's something else—I am a friend to me. I can play games or have discussions without involving people I don't like or don't want.

So, goodbye for now.

B: Perhaps I will meet you again.

C: Or, maybe you will meet me again.

A: Or, maybe you will meet all of us.

B: Just don't tell me that I have a split personality.

C: Because I'm just trying to be me.

A: And, that's enough for anyone,

B: or any two,

C: or any three.

Possible Extensions

1. Invite students to discuss the legal, moral, and ethical implications of human cloning. What might be some of the dangers? What might be some of the advantages? Do the advantages outweigh the dangers?

2. Cloning has been a science fiction topic for many years and is recently becoming more and more of a possibility for higher life-forms. Invite students to gather the latest information and scientific research about human cloning. How close are scientists to cloning humans?

3. Invite students to create a readers theatre script that takes place 50 years after the time of this script. What is different? Are there more clones in the world? What has happened to the characters in this script?

ALIEN TEACHER

Introduction

Teachers come in all shapes and sizes. Some might even come from distant worlds or faraway planets. You just never know!

Staging

The narrator can sit on a tall stool or stand behind a lectern or on a podium. The other characters should be standing and interacting with one another.

Student 1
X

Student 2
X

Student 3
X

Student 4
X

Student 5
X

Student 6
X

Narrator
X

Teacher
X

NARRATOR: It's the first day of school at Ganymede Middle School. Students have returned from summer vacation, and, while they are not eager to begin the new year, they are eager to catch up on all the latest news from their friends. They've also heard that there is a new teacher in the school. Nobody knows very much about this individual, but many of the students have the new teacher for their first period class. Some of them are afraid that the new teacher will be tough. Some are worried that the new teacher will give lots of

47

homework. Some aren't worried at all, but they're still very curious. Let's listen in on the conversation as this group of students waits for their new teacher.

STUDENT 1: I've never liked the first day of school. It's just too noisy, and there are too many meetings and assemblies and announcements all the time. It seems like everyone is running around being crazy, and nobody knows what they're doing or even what they're saying.

STUDENT 2: Hey, what do you think this new teacher will be like? Has anyone heard anything?

STUDENT 3: I heard that the school only hires really old teachers. They don't want to get any of those young teachers. I guess they think that the young teachers can't handle us. They probably think that we'd run all over them and give them lots of trouble and all that. So, they go out and find the oldest and meanest and grouchiest teachers they can.

STUDENT 4: Yeah, remember that teacher they hired a few years ago? Talk about being grouchy. All he did was scream. It sure kept us awake during class, but it wasn't much fun. They probably found that teacher living in some hole in the ground with all kinds of slimy creatures and weird stuff. I sure am glad that that teacher isn't back this year.

STUDENT 5: Remember the one they hired last year—the one who never looked at you? She would always be talking or saying something about history or science or something like that, but she never looked at you. Boy, that was spooky!

STUDENT 6: I'm not so sure about this school. There really are some weirdos here. I don't even know if I want to go here anymore. Oh, yeah, I know we have to—it's the law and all that, but when I look at some of the teachers here, it just freaks me out. I sometimes feel like one of them is going to come around the corner and zap me out. It's a strange place all right.

NARRATOR:	Just then the door to the classroom opens and in walks the new teacher. Everyone's jaws drop. They can't believe what they're seeing. It just doesn't seem possible.

The teacher walks in and stands off to the side of the staging area.

STUDENT 1:	*(Amazed)* Holy smokes! Will you take a look at that? I can't believe it!
STUDENT 2:	I've seen some strange teachers in my time, but never one like this!
STUDENT 3:	I just can't believe that the school would do something like this to us!
STUDENT 4:	Oh, no! It can't be.

The teacher walks to the chalkboard and writes, "Welcome from Miss Smith."

STUDENT 5:	*(Shocked)* You've got to be kidding me!
STUDENT 6:	*(Desperately)* This place is getting scarier and scarier all the time. Why did they have to do this? I tell you, it just isn't fair. Why us? Why us?
STUDENT 1:	This is unbelievable!
STUDENT 2:	It just isn't fair. It's not fair at all.
TEACHER:	Good morning, class. I'm Miss Smith, your new teacher. I'm really looking forward to working with all of you this year. There is so much to learn, and we're going to have a lot of fun.
STUDENT 3:	*(Whispering to Student 4)* Do you believe her?
STUDENT 4:	No way!
TEACHER:	Now, before I call roll, I'd like to tell you a little about myself.
STUDENT 5:	*(Whispering to Student 6)* Yeah, like that she's going to eat us for lunch!

STUDENT 6:   If we even live long enough to make it to lunch!

TEACHER: I grew up in a place called California. I lived in a small town on the ocean and spent my summers sailing and surfing. I went to school there and got my teaching degree. . . *(Her voice begins to trail off, becoming lower and lower.)*

NARRATOR: There in front of them was the new teacher they had all heard about. Yes, she was the ugliest teacher they had ever seen. Several students were feeling sick to their stomachs. No one knew what to say; everyone was speechless. They just couldn't believe what they were looking at. The new teacher had only two arms, two legs, and a single head. The students were shocked. For the first time in their lives their teacher was going to be a human being from the planet Earth.

Possible Extensions

1. Invite students to create a sequel to this script. What do Miss Smith's students learn about their new teacher that they didn't know before? What kinds of things does she make them do?

2. Invite students to discuss the classrooms of the future. What will they look like? How will they be designed? What teaching or learning tools will those classrooms have that are presently unavailable?

3. Divide students into several small groups. Invite each group to design the perfect teacher. For example, if they could order the ideal teacher (from a catalog, for example) what would that individual look like, what would that individual be able to do, and how would that individual be different from the teachers of today?

PART III

Goos, Brews, and Aliens Too

Introduction

We all have characteristics that are strengths for us. What would it be like if everybody's features were isolated and converted into a bag of slime? How could these characteristics be combined effectively to create the best possible individual?

Set-Up

Prior to this script, invite the actors to create some homemade "slime." What follows is a simple and basic recipe for slime. It's easy to make, but be sure students read through the entire recipe before they begin. Following the directions exactly as they are written will help ensure that they create the best possible slime.

Materials

1 sealable plastic sandwich bag or freezer bag

1 ounce of white glue (e.g., Elmer's Glue®)

3 to 4 drops of food coloring (red, green, yellow, blue)

2 ounces of water

½ teaspoon of borax (e.g., 20 Mule Team Borax®. This is used to help get clothes cleaner and can be found in the laundry section of your local grocery store).

Directions

1. Pour 1 ounce of white glue into the bottom of a plastic sandwich bag.

2. Drop in 2 or 3 drops of food coloring (red, green, yellow, or blue)

3. Pour in 1 ounce of water.

4. Use your hands to gently squish the sides of the sandwich bag together until the color is thoroughly mixed in (2 or 3 minutes). Set the bag aside for approximately 5 minutes.

5. Put ½ teaspoon of borax into a small cup or container.

6. Pour 1 ounce of water into the cup and stir the borax and water together with a spoon.

7. Quickly pour the borax and water into the plastic sandwich bag. (Because borax doesn't dissolve in the water, be sure that all the granules go into the bag. You may need to use the spoon to scrape out any leftover borax granules.) Seal the bag and begin to gently squish everything together.

8. Keep squishing until no liquid remains (3 to 5 minutes). While you're squishing, you'll notice that the ingredients are getting firmer and more "rubbery." (If there is still some liquid in the bag, sprinkle in just *a little bit* more borax and continue to squish until all the liquid is gone.)

9. Open the top of the bag and set it aside for 15 to 30 minutes. This allows some of the leftover liquid to evaporate and the chemical reaction to complete itself.

10. Now reach in and pull out a handful of homemade slime.

Important Notes

1. The amount of borax used in this recipe will determine the viscosity (thickness) of the slime. A little more borax, and the liquid will be thicker; a little less borax, and the liquid will be thinner.

2. Regular tap water or distilled water can be used for this recipe. Please be aware that tap water varies from place to place (the chemicals and/or minerals in the water differ from city to city and between urban and rural sources). These chemicals and minerals will affect the viscosity of your slime. You may need to compensate for the chemical composition of your own local water supply by adjusting the amount of borax used in the recipe.

3. Although borax is a common and frequently used laundry additive, students should note that there is a warning label on the side of the box. This means that they should never place borax or slime in or around their mouths.

4. Slime should be kept in a covered container. A plastic sandwich bag, a sealable freezer bag, or a food container with a sealable lid works best.

A Little Science

When white glue, borax, water, and food coloring are mixed together, slime is created. However, according to chemists, this mixture creates three things all at the same time: a colloid, a polymer, and a non-Newtonian fluid.

1. **Colloid.** A colloid is a mixture of two or more substances. A colloid could be a liquid in a liquid, a gas in a liquid, a solid in a liquid, a liquid in a solid, a gas in a solid, and so on. Slime is a colloid that combined a solid (borax) in a liquid (glue and water).

2. **Polymer.** A polymer is a specific type of colloid in which the molecules are all hooked together. Every substance in the universe has molecules. Usually, those molecules are floating around randomly inside the substance. Sometimes, when two (or more) substances are combined, the molecules get tangled with each other and form a complex web or net. This often creates a new substance, which in this case becomes harder and rubbery. We just call it slime (scientists call it a complex, cross-linked polymer).

3. **Non-Newtonian Fluid.** All fluids can flow. This flowing ability is called *viscosity*. Some liquids, such as molasses, have high viscosity (they're thick and flow slowly); other fluids, such as water, have low viscosity (they're thin and flow fast). When the viscosity of a liquid is affected by temperature it is called a *Newtonian fluid* (named after Sir Isaac Newton who, in the 1600s, discovered this principle). For example, pancake syrup could be called a Newtonian fluid because when it's heated, it flows faster; when it is cold from being in the refrigerator, it pours slowly. Applying a force can alter the viscosity of a non-Newtonian fluid. Students will notice that when they pull or push their slime it becomes just a little thicker and thus a little less able to flow. Its viscosity has been changed by something other than temperature.

Staging

The characters should all be standing in a loose group. They may wish to walk around the staging area as they talk with one another. Each character should have two or three small containers of slime (e.g., sandwich bags, paper cups, etc.). Preferably, each character will have a different color of slime, as noted below. There is no narrator for this script.

Student A (red)

X

Student B (green)   Student C (yellow)

X   X

Student D (blue)

X

STUDENT A: You know, I'm a little scared. We've all just come from the infirmary where they have processed parts of us into slime.

STUDENT B: You're right. It is a little scary. My protectors told me that when I reached the age of 10, I would have to go to the infirmary to be processed, but I really didn't know what they were talking about.

STUDENT C: Yeah, me too. I just thought it was something like getting pimples or changing your voice. I didn't realize that they turned some of your features into a bag of slime.

STUDENT D: Boy, I was really scared when I went in. They put a hood over my head and led me into an enormous whirring machine—almost like one of those washing machines they used to use many years ago, before disposable clothes. There were all kinds of noises and flashing lights that were so bright I could even see them through the hood.

STUDENT A: Yeah, me too. And what about the deathly silence that followed. I mean, I couldn't hear a thing. Nothing. It was as if all the sound in the world disappeared.

STUDENT B: Yeah, same here.

STUDENT C: And then a sharp piercing pain went through my brain from the left to the right side. Boy, that's when I was really scared. Good thing it only lasted for a few seconds. Then there was nothing.

STUDENT D:	Yeah. That's when I was led out of the machine and into a small room. I was told to sit down and wait. After about 10 minutes, a person wrapped in white tissue paper came out with this bag of slime *(holds up a bag for all to see)*.
STUDENT A:	Me too! And then the person gave me *The Tome* and told me to read it thoroughly. He said *The Tome* would have answers to all of my questions and would give me all the information I need to know.
STUDENT B:	So, here we are. We've all been to the infirmary, we've all gotten our bags of slime, and we've all read *The Tome*. I guess, now is the really scary part. Now we have to make The Decision.
STUDENT C:	That's right, The Decision. I just don't have any idea what I'm going to do.
STUDENT D:	I don't know. I'm still a little confused. How can they take some of the molecules in our bodies and convert them into a small bag of slime?
STUDENT A:	I guess it's part of the new technology. With space so limited on the planet, it was the only solution the Knowers could come up with. I guess it's lucky that the atomizer was invented.
STUDENT B:	What exactly does it do?
STUDENT C:	It converts atoms in your body. Brain cells, heart cells, foot cells, and fingernail cells are converted and miniaturized. What results is this bag *(holds bag up)* of slime. In other words, parts of us have been changed into an icky, gooey mass of slimy stuff.
STUDENT D:	I guess I understand that part, but what I don't understand is why each of us has a different color.
STUDENT A:	Well, according to *The Tome*, the atomizer is able to select the one quality, feature, or characteristic that is your strongest point. For example, you'll note *(holds bag up)* that my

slime is red. That means the atomizer determined that my strongest point is my intellectual ability—my brain power.

STUDENT B: So, what you're saying is that through some strange process that very few understand, the atomizer determines what you are best at, or what your strongest characteristic is, or what part of you is the best?

STUDENT C: That's right. For example, take a look at your slime's color. *(Student B holds the bag up.)* You're slime is green. That means your strongest characteristic is your athletic ability. It means the atomizer has determined that you have great physical strength and that this is your most well-developed feature. Now, if you take a look at my bag *(holds bag up)* you'll see that my slime is yellow. According to *The Tome*, that means my strongest point or most significant characteristic is my beauty. *(Everyone groans)* No, really! The atomizer has determined, through a careful analysis of my cellular structure, that my beauty exceeds every other characteristic of who I am.

STUDENT D: Now look at me. My slime is blue. When I read *The Tome* it said that blue means my most significant feature is my leadership ability.

STUDENT A: Well, this is very interesting. It's obvious that we all have different strengths and characteristics. But now comes the most difficult part of the whole process. We have to make The Decision.

STUDENT B: I know. But, how can we? None of us has any experience with this.

STUDENT C: Yeah. How can we make this important choice when we've never done it before?

STUDENT D: I guess it's the same for every Collection of Beings. They all had to do the same thing. They all had to decide without ever having any practice. They all had just one opportunity—right or wrong—just one opportunity.

STUDENT A:	Just like we do. There are no second chances. It's once and done!
STUDENT B:	That's really scary.
STUDENT C:	Yes it is! We must decide on the proportions of each of our slimes that will be used to create the Traveler.
STUDENT B:	Hey, just what are those Travelers?
STUDENT D:	Because of all the overcrowding here, it's been necessary during the last few centuries to send representatives—Travelers—to distant moons and star systems to populate the universe. Our planet couldn't hold any more, so the Knowers decided to limit the population here and to populate those distant places instead.
STUDENT A:	Yeah, and that's why we have the atomizer, and that's why we have to decide the amount of each slime to combine with the others to form one new Traveler. That Traveler will be placed on a new star and will be the vanguard of a new colony and a new population.
STUDENT B:	In short, we have to decide on the features this Traveler must have in order to make the new colony successful.
STUDENT C:	Wow, what a responsibility!
STUDENT D:	Yes, how much red should this new creation have? How much green? How much yellow? How much blue?
STUDENT A:	Do we want to create a Traveler who has lots of intellectual ability but very little beauty?
STUDENT B:	Do we want to create a Traveler who has a lot of athletic ability but very few leadership skills?
STUDENT C:	Or do we want to create a Traveler who has lots of beauty, a little bit of athletic skill, and some intellectual powers.

STUDENT D: I just don't know. There's too much to decide. We only have one chance. What skills, talents, and abilities should our new Traveler have that will help make it survive on the new star planet?

STUDENT A: Why don't we ask the Believers to help us?

STUDENT B: Okay. That sounds like a great idea!

STUDENT C: *(Addressing the audience)* Please help us make this decision. How much red, how much green, how much yellow and how much blue should we use to create the new Traveler?

STUDENT D: *(To the audience)* You will help us, won't you?

There is no ending to this script. At this point, invite the four actors to distribute small containers of slime to members of the audience. You may wish to engage the audience in one or more of the following extensions.

Possible Extensions

1. Divide the audience into several small groups. Invite each group to decide on the proportions of each color that should be used to create the Traveler. What feature or characteristic should dominate in the new individual?

2. Invite students to discuss the four features or characteristics that they think are most critical. If they were rewriting the script, what four features would they use in their production?

3. How do students feel about having some of their cells reduced to a bag of slime? What would be some of the advantages? What might be some disadvantages?

Introduction

If humans and aliens ever meet, how will they communicate. This script offers an interesting and unique approach to traditional forms of communication.

Set-Up

Prior to the presentation of this script, invite the actors to create a bubble solution. Following are five different recipes for bubbles. Invite students to experiment before-hand to determine which recipe works best (there are a variety of factors that will affect the quality of any bubble solution).

Materials

Recipe A. 1 cup of Joy® or Dawn® dishwashing liquid; 3 to 4 tablespoons glycerin (available in the hand-care section of a large drug store); 10 cups of cold water

Recipe B. 2 parts Joy® or Dawn® dishwashing liquid; (6 parts water; 4 parts glycerin

Recipe C. 8 ounces commercial bubble solution (e.g., Mr. Bubbles®); 1 ounce Joy® or Dawn®; 6 ounces water; 1 ounce glycerin

Recipe D. 2 parts Joy® or Dawn®; 1 part glycerin; 6 parts water; 8 parts commercial bubble solution

Recipe E. 6 parts water; 1 part Joy® or Dawn®; 1 part gelatin or glycerin

Important Notes

1. Always use distilled water. Tap water or well water typically contain too many impurities and/or particulate matter that will significantly shorten the longevity of the bubbles.

2. When selecting dishwashing liquid always choose Joy® or Dawn®. Other brands of dishwashing liquid will not work as well. Whenever possible, select the regular formulation, rather than the concentrated or super-concentrated solutions.

3. The best weather for bubble-making is cool and humid. Typically, the weather that immediately precedes a thunderstorm is the best. Days with high humidity and no wind are excellent bubble-making days.

4. Carbon dioxide will shorten the life of a bubble. Students should try to get as much air into their bubbles (rather than carbon dioxide) as possible.

5. Bubble blowing "machines" can be made from many common objects. One way is to take a common paper clip and straighten it out. Roll the end around your finger to create a closed loop with a short handle. Dip the loop into the bubble solution and blow. A second "machine" is a common rubber band. Wrap the rubber band around the thumb and index finger on one hand and the thumb and index finger on the other hand. Dip this into a container of bubble solution, lift it out, and blow. Invite students to create their own variations of bubble "machines" using a variety of household objects.

A Little Science

Everybody loves bubbles! They are great teaching tools and great entertainment all rolled into one. Here's some basic scientific information you might want to share with your students.

1. A bubble is defined as "encapsulated gas."

2. The reflection and refraction of light waves causes the colors in a bubble. The wall of a bubble has two sides—an outside surface and an inside surface. Although the sides are only a few millionths of an inch apart, they both reflect light back to the viewer. As the light waves come off these two surfaces, they interfere with each other. That interference causes the colors in the bubble (the same principle is in effect with rainbows). Interestingly, the thicker the wall of the bubble the more intense the colors. (Students can thicken their various bubble solutions by adding varying amounts of sugar.)

3. Bubbles are round because their walls are elastic—they are always pulling inward. This elasticity tries to enclose the air inside of it in the most efficient way possible. In nature, the most efficient geometric shape is a sphere simply because it has the least surface area of any geometric shape. Thus, bubbles are round.

4. Bubbles burst for several reasons. The chief causes of bubble-bursting are evaporation of the water in the bubble wall and particulate matter in the air or in the water used to make the bubbles.

Staging

There are two sets of characters for this script. The first set, positioned on the left side of the staging area, is human. These characters do all the talking. The second set, positioned on the right side of the staging area, is alien. They do no talking. However, throughout the reading of this script, they will be blowing bubbles (toward the humans) at specific times indicated by the word *Bubbles*. The narrator should stand at a lectern or on a podium at the side of the staging area.

Abby			Alien 1	
X			X	
Barry	Cathy		Alien 2	Alien 3
X	X		X	X

Narrator

X

NARRATOR:	The time is the present. The place is somewhere in the United States in a town very much like this town, except for one thing. Aliens have landed on the outskirts of town. Their craft is in an open field, and three of them have descended from it. The first humans to encounter these visitors from another world are three students *(sweeping his/her hand across the room)*—students very much like the students in this room. They are stunned by what they see but know that this is a critical time. They are not sure if the aliens are friendly or if they came prepared for war. They are not sure how long the aliens plan to stay or what their intentions are. They realize that what they say now, before the military surrounds this little spot of land, may well determine not only their fate, but the fate of many other humans as well.
ABBY:	Hey, guys. Look at that! Three aliens just came down the ramp of that spacecraft and are standing right there! What do we do?
BARRY:	First of all, let's be real careful. We don't know if they are friendly or not. For all we know they could have some sort

of ray gun and just zap us like that. POOF! And we'd be nothing but a pile of ashes somewhere in the middle of America.

Bubbles

CATHY: Hey, what did they just do? What are they doing?

ABBY: I don't know. Maybe we should run for it.

BARRY: Yeah, maybe we should. But look, they're not doing anything. They're not pulling out any ray guns or atomic weapons or anything like that. They're just standing there staring at us. But maybe they're just sizing us up and then will take over our bodies, and we'll be turned into big gooey sloppy blobs of protoplasm!

CATHY: I think you've been watching too many late-night movies. Those aliens sure don't look like they're going to shoot us or anything.

Bubbles

ABBY: Look, they did it again. I wonder what's going on. All they do is stand there, stare at us, and make all those bubbles. It's kinda spooky.

BARRY: You know what? If they're aliens they probably come from another planet.

CATHY: (*Sarcastically*) Bright deduction, Sherlock!

BARRY: No, listen. If you traveled to some foreign country where you've never been before wouldn't you have some difficulties?

ABBY: What do you mean?

BARRY: Look, if you went to France, how would you know what to say? How would you communicate if you had never spoken French before?

CATHY:	Well, I'd probably try to draw some pictures, or maybe I'd try to use some hand signals or something like that.
BARRY:	Yeah, right. That's exactly what you would do.

Bubbles

ABBY:	There they go again. They're really making me nervous.
BARRY:	Just wait a minute. Let's pretend for a second that these aliens are trying to communicate with us.
CATHY:	*(Sarcastically)* Oh, sure! They're trying to communicate by blowing bubbles at us.
BARRY:	Now hold on. Just think about it. They certainly don't speak any English, and for all we know they probably don't speak any language that we're familiar with. I'm sure they have their own form of communication just like we have our own form of communication.
ABBY:	*(Somewhat sarcastically)* Wow, maybe "Bright Boy" is starting to make some sense.
CATHY:	Yeah, maybe he is. So what you're saying, Barry, is that these creatures or aliens are trying to communicate with us through the only way they know how—bubbles.
BARRY:	That's it exactly. Look, the way we are communicating—using our mouths and making strange sounds that we call words might be really weird to them. For all we know, we may be the first human beings they have ever seen. They're certainly the first aliens we have ever seen.

Bubbles

ABBY:	Okay, I guess you're starting to make some sense. But it does give us one major problem—how are we going to communicate with them. How will they be able to understand us and how will we be able to understand them?
BARRY:	Yeah, I guess we have a real problem on our hands.

CATHY: You bet we do. I wonder if they are getting as frustrated with this whole thing as we are.

Bubbles

BARRY: I don't know, but it does seem as though they are making an honest effort to try to communicate with us. Obviously we can't understand what they are trying to say, but at least we know they're friendly.

ABBY: And weird!

CATHY: Not so fast. They may look strange, but we probably look pretty strange to them. After all, like Barry said, they're probably having the same communication problems we are.

ABBY: So what can we do?

Bubbles

BARRY: I think I've got it! I think I've got a way to communicate with the aliens! Watch me!

Barry takes a bubble wand and dips it into some bubble solution. He gently blows some bubbles toward the aliens. When he does, the aliens' faces light up with big smiles.

ABBY: Look. Look what's happening. I think Barry has found the answer.

CATHY: I think you're right. Why don't we do it, too?

All three of the humans dip bubble wands into a bubble solution and gently blow their bubbles toward the aliens. The aliens respond by blowing more bubbles toward the humans.

NARRATOR: And so, on a sunlit day somewhere in the middle of America, two completely different civilizations came together for the first time. With nothing in common and with no language that could be understood by both, they invented a form of communication. It was an historic meeting—one that did not involve guns or weapons or planes or ships or rockets. It simply involved two different species inventing a form of communication that brought both happiness and joy to all the participants. It was the first time these two civilizations had ever communicated, and it was a communication filled with joy and laughter and understanding.

Possible Extensions

1. Invite students to write a sequel to this script. What might these two species do in the future? What would happen if adults, with their sophisticated forms of communication, tried to interact with the aliens? Would those meetings be as friendly?

2. Invite students to investigate various forms of communication used throughout the world. These could include (but are not limited to) sign language, dance, facial expressions, smoke signals, etc. Why have humans developed so many different forms of communication?

3. Students may wish to create their own readers theatre script about the first meeting between humans and aliens. Where will it take place? What will be some of the important events? What will be the eventual outcome?

I SCREAM, YOU SCREAM, WE ALL SCREAM FOR ICE CREAM

Introduction

Everybody loves ice cream. It tastes good and keeps you cool in hot weather. But, if you're not careful, it can also do something else to you, something quite unexpected.

Set-Up

During the course of this script, students are asked to create some homemade ice cream. Below is a basic recipe for ice cream that is easy to make. Be sure to provide all the students in your class with copies of this recipe so they can share it with family members. This recipe will produce enough ice cream for one or two small servings. Adjust it to the number of students in the class.

Materials

1 gallon sealable freezer bag

1 pint sealable freezer bag

1 spoon

2 cups (approximately) of ice (small cubes or cracked)

6 tablespoons of salt

1 tablespoon of sugar

½ teaspoon of vanilla

½ cup of whole milk

Directions

1. Put the ice into the large freezer bag. Pour the salt over the ice in the bag. Set this large bag aside for a few moments.

2. Pour the milk into the small freezer bag. Add the sugar and vanilla to the milk. Mix the ingredients thoroughly. (The bag can be squished by hand for 20 to 30 seconds.)

3. Remove some of the air from the small freezer bag and seal it tightly.

4.   Place the small freezer bag inside the large freezer bag. Seal the large freezer bag.

5.   Place the large freezer bag on a flat surface (e.g., table top, kitchen counter) and turn it over and over (by the corners) for approximately five minutes.

6.   Carefully open the large freezer bag and remove the small freezer bag.

7.   Wipe off the top of the small freezer bag and open it.

8.   Spoon out some of the homemade ice cream and enjoy!

Important Notes

1.   Be sure to use whole milk only. The recipe will not work with skim milk or other types of reduced fat milk.

2.   Always use name-brand freezer bags. Generic freezer bags might not be completely sealed around the edges and might leak during the activity.

3.   Students might want to experiment later by adding different flavors to the basic recipe. Suggested flavors include peppermint, cinnamon, or cherry. Students might also wish to add chocolate chips or coconut sprinkles to their ice cream creations. Add different food colors to create colorful ice cream (e.g., blue ice cream).

A Little Science

Combine whole milk, some flavoring, some sweetener, and a freezing agent (ice) and you have ice cream (a crude form, to be sure). The formation of ice cream (the commercial variety) is detailed below:

1.   A mixture of dairy ingredients such as fresh milk, cream, buttermilk, or whey is formulated.

2.   Sugars are added.

3.   Stabilizers are added in order to prevent the formation of ice crystals.

4.   The ice cream mixture is pasteurized at 79 degrees Celsius (C) (175 degrees Fahrenheit [F]) for 25 seconds.

5.   The heated mix is homogenized to ensure its smoothness.

6.   The mix is then cooled to 4.4 degrees C (40 degrees F) for at least four hours. This allows the fat to solidify.

7.   The mix is partially frozen and air is whipped into it.

8.   The semifrozen ice cream is placed in a blast freezer where the temperature is rapidly lowered to between minus 9 degrees and minus 5 degrees C (16 to 23 degrees F). This rapid freezing prevents the formation of ice crystals (something that will be present in the homemade ice cream described above).

9.   The ice cream is then transferred to a hardening room where the internal temperature is lowered even further to a core temperature of minus 18 degrees C (0 degrees F). It is then ready for shipping.

Staging

The characters can be standing, or they can be seated on tall stools. There is no narrator for this script. Instead, the character Baldor directs the flow. The character Legnon does nothing and says nothing until the end of the script.

Baldor	Ann	Bob	Carrie	Doug	Legnon
X	X	X	X	X	X

Empty chairs
X   X   X   X

Invite the actors to each make a batch of homemade ice cream. Each batch should be in a separate sealable freezer bag. Provide Baldor with all five bags of ice cream to begin the production.

ANN: *(To Baldor)* Hey, you must be the new kid.

BALDOR: That's right. I just got into town and this is my first day at school. I just wanted to be friendly, so I thought I would get you guys some of this frozen dessert. *(Passes the bags of ice cream out to each actor)* Go ahead, try some.

Each actor, including Baldor, begins to eat the ice cream.

BOB: Hey, this stuff is good. Thanks a lot.

CARRIE: Yeah, thanks a lot. Boy, there's nothing like some good old fashioned ice cream on a hot day.

BALDOR: Is that what you call this stuff—ice cream?

DOUG: Yeah, what else would you call it? It's just plain old ice cream. It keeps you cool in the summer and sure does taste good.

BALDOR: You enjoy the flavor?

ANN: Yeah, I can't remember when I've had ice cream this good. Did this come from Jake's Ice Cream Stand?

BALDOR: No, it came from a very special place, and it has very special properties.

BOB: What do you mean it has very special properties? The only properties I can see are that it's cold and it's good. What else is there?

BALDOR: I am sure that in a very short time you will discover some special properties of this ice cream that you have never experienced before.

CARRIE: What do you mean "never experienced before"?

The characters (except Baldor and Legnon) are slowly becoming sluggish. Their speech patterns are slowed down and their movements are very measured and controlled.

BALDOR: Are you noticing that you are talking a little slower than you normally do? That you are moving slower than you normally do? That's fine. Do not be worried. Everything is fine.

DOUG: What's happening? What is happening to my body? My body is feeling slower. I'm getting slower.

ANN: I'm having trouble thinking. I can't think as fast as I usually do. What is happening?

BALDOR: Nothing. Nothing at all. Nothing is happening to you that we don't want to happen.

BOB: What do you mean "we"?

BALDOR: Oh, nothing. Nothing to be worried about. Nothing at all to be worried about.

CARRIE: I'm not worried. I'm feeling just fine. I'm a little slower than I used to be, but I'm just fine.

DOUG: I feel like I'm very sleepy. I feel just like I do after I take an exam . . . a hard exam that I had to study for the whole night before. That's what I feel like.

BALDOR: That's good. You're feeling just fine. The ice cream, as you call it, is very very good. It helps you feel just fine. It helps you feel good.

In the next section, each character says something. After speaking, each character's head slumps forward onto his or her chest. They appear to be in a trances. Each time a character's head falls forward Baldor and Legnon lead that character over to an empty chair and place the individual into the chair. Baldor and Legnon do this until all four characters are in chairs.

ANN: *(Very slowly)* I like ice cream. I like ice cream very much. Very much I like ice cream. Ice cream is good. *(Head slumps, and she is lead to a chair where she sits down.)*

BOB: *(Slowly)* I like ice cream. I like ice cream very much. Very much I like ice cream. Ice cream is good. *(Head slumps, and he is lead to a chair where he sits down.)*

CARRIE: *(Slowly)* I like ice cream. I like ice cream very much. Very much I like ice cream. Ice cream is good. *(Head slumps, and she is lead to a chair where she sits down.)*

DOUG: *(Slowly)* I like ice cream. I like ice cream very much. Very much I like ice cream. Ice cream is good. *(Head slumps and he is lead to a chair where he sits down.)*

BALDOR: Now, my new friends, you will listen to me. You have eaten some of the magic potion—the food you Earthlings call ice cream. However, it is much more than a frozen treat. It is a substance created by the scientists on my world—Quasar VII. We are a more advanced form of life than you. We have perfected interstellar travel. We are able to travel great distances through space in a short amount of time. Thus, we have been able to visit many stars and many planets throughout the universe. We have, in fact, been visiting your planet for many years, observing your habits and observing your ways. Because we are a much higher form of life, we have also learned your language—English. We are able to converse as though we have been speaking English for all of our lives.

LEGNON: We are different in another way. While you assume large forms, forms with arms and legs and bodies, we do not. In fact, our structures are far smaller than yours. We are at the molecular level in size. We are so small that we cannot be seen by your eyes—not even by the instruments you call microscopes. We are some of the smallest particles in the entire universe. That is how we are able to travel vast distances in a relatively short amount of time.

BALDOR: Our world—Quasar VII—is in great danger. It has been knocked out of its orbit and will crash into the planet you call Jupiter in less than three months. Thus, several of us have been sent to your world to scout it as a possible new planet for our civilization. We have found many things that we like about your world. But there is one part of your world that is very difficult for us. It is a world full of large things—large bodies and large people. We are small—so small that we could not exist in this kind of environment. So, our brilliant scientists have devised an ingenious method that allows us to survive, and ice cream is the key!

LEGNON: Because Quasar VII is so far away from the sun, it is a cold frozen world. We are happy in that environment, but soon that environment will cease to exist. Our scientists have made it possible for us to survive on your world by being some of the molecules in ice cream—a substance that is the same temperature as on Quasar VII. But the brilliance of our scientists did not stop there, for when that ice cream is eaten by any human being, we can become that human being. We can take on the size and shape of that human being. We can have arms and legs like that human being. We can have a head and a body just like that human being. In fact, we *are* that human being. We now can live. We now can survive. Each time a human eats the substance you call ice cream, that human is ingesting one of us. One of us is taking over that person. One of us will be that person. One more of us will be able to survive. That human being will no longer exist. That human being will be one of us. WE WILL BE YOU! WE ARE YOU!

BALDOR:	Now, my friends, raise your heads. *(They all look up at Baldor.)* Although you are still in your original bodies, you are no longer you. You are one of us. Soon we will have invaded all of the bodies on Earth, and then this planet will be our planet, and we will create a great and majestic civilization.
ANN:	Hey, guys, did that ice cream make you sleepy like it did me?
BOB:	Yeah, it sure did. It also made me feel a little different, you know, a little strange.
CARRIE:	Yeah, me too. I mean, I'm still in the same body, but I just don't feel like me.
DOUG:	Boy, this is really weird.
BALDOR:	Welcome comrades. Welcome to our new world.
ANN:	*(Pointing to audience)* Hey, what about those people there?
BOB:	Yeah, maybe we should be good hosts and offer them some of this terrific ice cream.
CARRIE:	You're right. Let's make some right now and share it with all our friends.
DOUG:	Let's go! Come on everyone, let's make some terrific ice cream. It tastes great. And it may even change your life!

The class can all participate in creating their own individual portions of homemade ice cream while discussing or participating in one or more of the following extensions.

Possible Extensions

1. Several movies and science fiction stories have postulated that alien beings have landed on the planet Earth and have taken the form of humans. Invite students to engage in a spirited discussion about the implications of that possibility. What do they think the aliens would want to do first when they assume human forms? How would they eventually take over the world?

2.   Invite students to create their own readers theatre script as a sequel to this script. What do the four characters do during the course of the next several days? Weeks? Months? How will they interact with their peers? How will they interact with their families? Will they try to get everyone to eat some ice cream?

3.   If students could assume any shape or form (real or imaginary), what shape would they want to be? Would they take the form of an animal, or would they want to create something that has never been seen before? What would be some of the advantages of the new form(s)?

IT'S IN THE BAG

Introduction

Many things can be found inside an innocent-looking bag. Sometimes you might even find one of the strangest life forms ever!

Set-Up

This script takes place over the course of three days. Students will create a simulation of a natural and normal process in nature—decomposition. You may wish to use this script in concert with a science lesson on decomposition or a unit on a specific environment (e.g., the rainforest, deciduous forests).

Materials

4 one-pint, sealable plastic sandwich bags

2 packets of yeast

4 small, ripe bananas

1 table knife

Water

Directions

1. Label each bag with a letter (A, B, C, and D)

2. Unpeel a banana. Cut off the two ends. Slice the rest of the banana into 3 or 4 equally sized pieces.

3. Place the slices of banana into Bag A, seal it, and set it aside.

4. Slice a second banana and place 3 or 4 slices inside Bag B.

5. Pour the contents from one packet of yeast into Bag B, seal the bag, and set aside.

6. Slice a third banana and place 3 or 4 slices inside Bag C.

7. Pour approximately ¼ cup of water into Bag C, seal the bag, and set aside.

8. Slice the fourth banana and place 3 or 4 slices inside Bag D.

9. Pour one packet of yeast and ¼ cup of water into Bag D, seal the bag, and set aside.

10.   Place the bags in a warm location (e.g., sunny windowsill, radiator)

11.   Observe the contents of the bags for any changes.

Important Notes

1.   Always use name-brand sandwich bags. Generic sandwich bags may not be completely sealed around the edges. This will cause leaking during the activity.

2.   You may wish to adjust the amount of water poured into each bag. Depending on the source of water (city water, well water, bottled spring water), there may be more or less minerals and other particulate matter in the water. This will affect the decomposition process taking place inside the bags.

3.   For the best results, use very ripe bananas (rich yellow skin just beginning to turn black).

4.   Transfer the yeast into small, unlabeled containers in advance of this activity. Have the bananas peeled and set up in advance of the activity, too.

A Little Science

This activity demonstrates the process of decomposition, a normal process that takes place in nature all the time. Decomposition is the action of microorganisms that break down organic materials so they are returned to the earth. Were it not for decomposition, we would be overwhelmed by mountains of garbage and other refuse. In this activity, each of the four bags demonstrates partial or complete decomposition as follows:

1.   In Bag A the banana slices will darken. This is due to the small amount of air that was trapped in the bag when it was sealed. The banana slices may darken completely or just slightly depending on the quantity of air in the bag.

2.   In Bag B the yeast will grow slowly, but there will be little change. Yeast is a plant and will use the little bit of moisture in the banana slices to begin its growth process. It won't be able to complete the growth process because of the limited moisture.

3.   In Bag C there will be decay and mold development after a period of three days. The air and water will provide some of the environmental conditions necessary for decomposition to begin, but without a necessary biological agent, the process will not continue.

4.   In Bag D there will be the greatest change. After three days, the banana will be decomposing significantly. The liquid may be bubbling and carbon dioxide (a by-product of the decomposition process) will be forming inside the bag. The bag will swell and may even pop open from the internal pressure. If so, a foul odor (rotting organic material) will pervade the area. Bag

D demonstrates, much more rapidly than in nature, the process of decomposition. Air, water, and a decomposer (yeast) are all present on a type of organic matter (the banana). These conditions—not present in the other three bags—are ideal for decomposition. This activity is important because students are able watch a "high speed" version of the decomposition process inside a mini-environment (a clear sandwich bag). Students need to understand that, in nature, this process may take several months or years depending on the materials. A dead tree, for example, may take many years to decompose in the forest; while a mouse's body may decompose in a matter of weeks.

Production Note

This script can be presented in one of two ways. It can be performed over a period of three days as outlined below, or students may wish to create three separate sets of the four banana bags—the first set created two days in advance of the production, the second set created the day before the production, and the third set created on the same day as the production. Each set of bags can then be used to illustrate the various stages of the decomposition process all at one time. The second set of bags replaces the third set during the "Day Two" part of the production; the first set of bags replaces the second set during the "Day Three" part of the production.

Staging

The characters can all be standing or can sit on tall stools. There should be a small table in front of the characters. All the supplies listed above should be on the table. There is no narrator for this script. All the characters should talk in monotones or in a "robotic" style of presentation.

22	83	31	56
X	X	X	X

Day One

22:   Well, my friends, it looks like our mission is quite successful. We have obtained the necessary samples that we came for (points to the four peeled bananas on the table).

83: You are right, 22, we have been extremely successful. When this mission began, I did not think it would go as well as it has.

31: We were fortunate to have stumbled on so many specimens at the same time. Remember, when we started off, Mission Central said we might not find all the specimens that we hoped for. This, I believe, has exceeded our wildest dreams.

56: So true, so true. And to think that we were able to obtain these without a struggle or a fight. I must say, the specimens were quite complacent. They did not put up any resistance. It was much more than we could have hoped for.

22: You are right, 56, these specimens were much easier to trap than those we have encountered in other places.

83: Yes, I remember the time we found the small furry creatures in the green place. We had to spend much time running about to capture just one of those creatures. It was very strenuous, and we only obtained a single sample.

31: Yes, there have been many journeys and many explorations where we have obtained nothing, nothing at all. But this time is different. We have made our greatest capture ever.

56: I agree, but now we must begin the experiment. Now we will learn whether we have captured a great and noble quarry or a worthless and meaningless sample. Let us begin.

22: I will take this specimen *(picks up a peeled banana)* and remove several samples from it. *(Using a dull table knife, 22 cuts several slices off the end of the banana.)* I'm going to place these into one of the Experiment Containers *(places the banana slices into Bag A)* and carefully seal the container. Now we may watch what happens inside *(seals bag and sets it aside)*. 83, you may now begin your portion of the experiment.

83:   Yes. I will use this second sample *(places the second peeled banana on the table)*. First I am going to slice several samples from it *(cuts three or four slices off the end of the banana)*. Now I will place these samples into an Experiment Container *(places the slices inside Bag B)*. Next I will add the Life Grains *(pours the unmarked container of yeast into the bag)*. Now I will set this experiment aside and watch it closely.

31:   It is time for me to begin the third phase of the experiment. I will prepare some slices from the third sample *(places the third peeled banana on the table)*. I'm going to use this blade to remove several slices *(uses the knife to cut three or four slices off of the banana)*. These samples will go into the third Experiment Container *(places the slices inside Bag C)*. I must carefully handle this Crystal Elixir and add some of it to the Experiment Container *(pours about one-fourth cup of water into the bag and seals it)*. Now I will place this experiment near the other two so that we can observe and compare them.

56:   I will handle the final portion of the experiment *(places the fourth peeled banana on the table)*. As all of you have done before me, I will remove several slices from the sample *(cuts three or four slices from the banana)*. Next, I must put these samples into the final Experiment Container *(places the slices into Bag D)*. I must also pour the mixture of Life Grains into the container *(pours the sample of yeast into the bag)*. As it is explained in the instruction manual, I will also pour in a small portion of the Crystal Elixir *(pours about one-fourth cup of water into the bag and seals it)*. Now I'll place this experiment with all the others.

22:   According to the instruction manual, we must wait.

Day Two

31 picks up the bags and examines them carefully.

56:   This experiment takes much time. It is slow to develop.

83:   Yes, you are right, but it is a much better process than what we used in the Old Times. Do you remember how we had to wait for many passings of the yellow orb across the sky?

22:   Yes. They say that those were the "good days," but I think we didn't know very much then. Now, our processes and our experiments are sophisticated, we can learn much more from the samples we collect.

56:   I agree. In fact, let's look at the Experiment Containers to see if they reveal any of the information we need.

22:   Look at the sample I prepared *(holds Bag A up for all to see)*. It has changed color. The color of the sample has become darker. I guess we all know what that means.

Everyone nods their head.

83:   Now I want to look at the samples I placed in my Experiment Container *(holds up Bag B)*. If you look closely, you will see that the samples have made very little change. It is just as we thought it would be.

31:   I am looking at the samples I placed in this bag *(holds up Bag C)*. I can see that there is some decay and some discoloration on the samples. I must consult the exploration manual to determine what this means *(goes to another section of the staging area to read a large book)*. Oh, now I see what this is.

56:   Let us examine the contents of my Experiment Container. *(Picks up Bag D and looks carefully inside. Scratches head and looks puzzled by the contents of the bag.)* I do not know what I am seeing here. This is something unusual. I must look at the Exploration Manual to determine what is happening *(begins to read over the shoulder of 31 in a very puzzled manner)*.

22:   Some of the results are what we expected them to be.

83:   And, some of the results are not what we expected them to be.

31:   It seems we must do more work, more research, more investigation before we can truly know what these samples represent in this new world on which we landed.

Everyone continues to look into their bags with amused (22 and Bag A), serious (83 and Bag B), alarmed (31 and Bag C), and confused (56 and Bag D) expressions on their faces.

Day Three

22:   I have carefully examined the contents of my Experiment Container. Through a careful analysis and thorough research paradigm, I've been able to determine where this sample came from.

83:   Well, 22 what did you discover?

22:   I have no doubt that these *(holds up Bag A)* are slices of brain tissue from a small, black and white, furry animal that lives in wooded areas. I believe it is what the inhabitants of this planet refer to as a skunk.

83:   Very good, 22. I have been equally successful in analyzing the samples that were in my Container *(holds up Bag B)*. After my analysis and examination of these samples, I can now conclude that they are sections of a brain from that of a large aquatic animal called "shark" by the inhabitants of this strange new world.

31:   That is excellent, 83. We have all made very interesting discoveries. As I carefully examined my container and read all the field notes that the High Command sent with us, I have concluded that this bag *(holds up Bag C)* has samples of brain matter from a creature that is sometimes referred to as a grizzly bear.

22:   56, you still look very confused. *(Pointing to Bag D)* Have you been able to determine what your samples are?

56:   I believe I have. It was very difficult trying to learn about these samples. I watched this bag very carefully and noted in my log book that the liquid inside was bubbling. I also saw that there was a lot of gas building up inside the container. A lot of bubbles and a lot of gas. At first I wasn't sure what the sample was.

83: But you did know that they were slices of brain matter from a creature that lives on this new world?

56: Yes, I did. I had to rule out many possibilities and many options. I spent much time reading reference materials in the mother ship's library. But it finally came down to one and only one possibility.

31: What was it that let you know?

56: I guess it was all the gas that was being released from the brain samples. I saw all that gas inside the experiment container and suddenly, I knew what it was.

22: So, what is it?

56: I am convinced that it could only be one thing—these *(holds up bag)* only can be brain samples from a creature known as a TEENAGER!

Possible Extensions

1. If possible, obtain a video (from the National Geographic Society or the Discovery Channel) about the human brain. Invite students to share and discuss what they learn from the video(s). They may want to set up a special display in the classroom outlining important sections of the human brain or comparing a human brain to an animal brain.

2. Invite students to create a sequel to this script. What other items could this band of four explorers look at? What items would provide them with the most information or background data about the possible inhabitants of a distant world?

3. How do students feel about having someone (or something) look at slices of their brains? Which portions would they want to have examined (assuming they would have a choice)?

PART IV

Search for Knowledge

ALL THE KNOWLEDGE IN THE UNIVERSE

Introduction

What if you could swallow one small pill and gain all the knowledge in the universe? Would you? What might be the consequences? This script looks at those questions, but doesn't offer any easy solutions.

Staging

The narrator may sit on a stool or stand at a lectern at the side of the staging area. The characters should all be standing in a loose-knit group. They can occasionally move around as they are speaking to each other. NOTE: A small prop is needed for this production—a peppercorn, peanut, or raisin can serve as the "intelli-pod."

Kay   Marti
X   X

  Seth   Jennifer
  X   X

Narrator
X

NARRATOR: The time is the present, the place is just outside [insert the name of your local high school and town]. Here we find four friends who are talking about the day, their classes, and the future. It is just an average day, a day that is neither special nor unusual . . . except for the fact that these four people will be changed by a small, seemingly insignificant item about which they must make one of the most difficult decisions of their young lives. Their decision will shape their futures just as much as it will shape this day—an otherwise average day that is neither special nor unusual.

87

KAY: Hey, guys! What's going on?

MARTI: Nothing much. I'm on my way over to Burgerville to flip some burgers and make a couple of bucks. What about you?

SETH: Oh, I don't know. Maybe I'll just hang out for a while. Hey, Jenn, what's that you've got there?

JENNIFER: *(Holding an "intelli-pod" in her hand)* It's called an intelli-pod. You guys probably have seen these on TV. My parents went ahead and ordered one—it cost them a lot of money, but I guess they wanted to help me out with school and all that. I think they're only sold to a few, select people in the country . . . *(hesitantly)* but I'm not so sure I want it.

KAY: What do you mean, you're not sure?

JENNIFER: Well, you see, these things have all the knowledge in the universe built into them. My parents figure that if I have one of these things implanted in my head I can get good grades, get into college, and maybe get a decent job when I graduate. Like, not flipping burgers.

MARTI: *(Indignant)* Hey, I resent that.

JENNIFER: Well, resent it or not, my parents think that this could be the thing that turns my life around. If I had it inserted into my head, I'd never have to worry about anything. I could discover the answers to every question on a test. I would know the most complex mathematical equations and chemical formulas. I could know the cure for cancer, the cure for the common cold, the cures for every single disease on the face of the Earth. I could know the answers for eliminating poverty, starvation, and homelessness around the world. I would know everything about the planets and the universe. In short, I would know everything about everything.

SETH: Wow, that sounds like a lot of knowledge! Just think, to be able to know everything about everything . . . wouldn't that impress everyone?

MARTI:	Yeah! That would be great. Scientists would be asking you for all the answers to their problems. Politicians would be asking you to solve international conflicts. The folks on Wall Street would be asking you to eliminate financial problems. Just think—you could be the font of all knowledge. Everybody would be coming to you for the answer to any question they might have.
KAY:	Gee, Jenn, that sounds great. You must be pretty excited. So, when are you going to have the operation?
JENNIFER:	I'm not so sure I'm going to do it.
SETH:	What do you mean? You'd be giving up one of the greatest opportunities of all time.
MARTI:	Why wouldn't you? This sounds like an easy decision. You just go into your doctor's office and you come out with more power than any other individual on the planet. You'd be Miss Smarts—the genius of the universe.
JENNIFER:	*(Tentatively)* Yeah, I guess so.
KAY:	So, why the long face? It's a "no-brainer!" You would be the chosen one. For example, I'd choose you to sit next to me during that algebra test that Miss Crimmins is giving next week.
JENNIFER:	Yeah, I guess so. But you see, the intelli-pod is complete and total knowledge—complete and total knowledge about everything. *(Emphatically)* That's *everything!*
KAY:	What are you trying to say?
JENNIFER:	For example, *(pointing to Kay)* I would know the exact time and day that *you* are going to die. *(Pointing to Seth)* I would know the exact time and day that *you* are going to die. *(Pointing to Marti)* I would know the exact time and day that *you* are going to die.

SETH: Hey, Jenn, don't get so serious on us. Slow down, take it easy!

MARTI: Jenn, you're scaring us. Are you saying that this intelli-pod also gives you the power to read the future?

JENNIFER: Yeah! I'd know the past, the present, *and* the future! I would know things about you that not even you would know about you.

KAY: Boy, that's really scary. You mean you would know who we are going to marry, what our children will look like, what kinds of houses we're going to live in? Would you know all that stuff?

JENNIFER: Yeah! But even more than that, I would know about every airplane crash that would happen—even before it happened. I would know about every battle and war and about all the people who would be killed and how they would be killed. I would know about every hurricane or earthquake and all the damage they would do. Yes, guys, I would know everything.

SETH: Would you know if I was going to get cancer or something like that?

JENNIFER: Yeah!

MARTI: Would you know if I was going to get into a car accident and be severely injured?

JENNIFER: Yeah!

KAY: Would you know if I was going to spend my life in a homeless shelter and have to beg for food on the street?

JENNIFER: Yeah! I would know all that. You see, the intelli-pod is complete and total knowledge of everything. It would not only give me the knowledge of things that are happening right now—like the fact that Seth's stomach is gurgling and he wants to go down to Burgerville and get a couple of burgers—but it also would give me the knowledge of things and events that would happen tomorrow, or next week, or even in the next century.

MARTI: Wow, that is scary.

KAY: So, what are you going to do?

SETH: Yeah, what are you going to do?

MARTI: WHAT . . . ARE . . . YOU . . . GOING . . . TO . . . DO?

NARRATOR: Ladies and gentlemen, it seems as though our friend Jennifer has a very difficult decision on her hands. In fact, in her hand *(pointing to the intelli-pod)* she holds the power of the universe—all the knowledge that she, or the rest of humanity would ever need. Right there *(pointing again)* in her hand is complete and *total* knowledge, but she is having difficulty making her decision. So, I will turn it over to you. What do you think? What would you do? If you could have all the knowledge in the universe, would you want it?

Possible Extensions

1. Invite the audience to discuss the implications and ramifications of complete and total knowledge. What would it mean? What types of power would it give an individual? Students may wish to organize themselves into two groups to debate the matter.

2. Invite a small group of students to craft a sequel to this script. What would happen to Jennifer the next day if she went ahead and had the intelli-pod implanted in her head?

3. Invite students to make a list of some of the knowledge they would like to have, as well as a list of knowledge they would rather not have. Which list is longer?

Introduction

Will there ever be a time when the human brain becomes useless? Will computers ever take over our thinking and reasoning powers? Will we ever allow something like that to happen? These are not easy questions to answer, but this script asks them nonetheless.

Staging

The four characters stand around a small table. There should be a computer or computer monitor on the table. The narrators may stand on podiums or at lecterns at the front of the staging area.

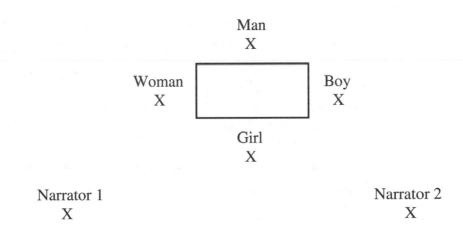

NARRATOR 1:   It is almost the end of the twenty-first century. The location is anywhere—a land of wise and intelligent beings who seek the greatest knowledge the world has to offer. They are beings who are able to keep that knowledge in small places and small compartments. Sometimes they share this knowledge with others; sometimes they save it for themselves. Every time their knowledge increases, they are able to place more in the special compartments that occupy every corner in this land of wise and intelligent beings.

NARRATOR 2:   In this land, all the knowledge of the world has been compacted into the "Compartments of Knowledge." Indeed, *all* the knowledge of the world is assigned to the Compartments, and they are overflowing with wisdom and erudition. In this land, the people have no knowledge, for they have assigned their knowledge to the Compartments. It is the Compartments that do all of the thinking and make all of the decisions for the people. The people have released the powers of thinking and all the knowledge of the world to the Compartments. There is a silence throughout the land.

NARRATOR 1:   But, *all* is not silent. In a small corner of a small village in a small region in the southwest corner of the land, a small band of people have gathered. And they talk.

WOMAN: *(Frowning)* I am worried. We have lost our knowledge. We do not think like we did in the past.

BOY: Yes, there is much emptiness. It is difficult for us to do anything unless we are led by a Compartment of Knowledge.

GIRL: You are right. In the old days we could think and reason. Our people were able to solve problems and figure out answers. That is what the old people have told us.

MAN: Yes. Our heads are not full as they once were. It is very difficult to do anything for ourselves. I do not know what we will do. These are very difficult days for us.

BOY: *(Walking toward the man)* Tell us, how was it in the old days? What was it like?

MAN: *(Sadly)* It was much different. According to the legends of the wise ones, our people were once thinkers. Many thousands of years ago they lived in large buildings and traveled in moving vehicles. For reasons no one can remember, our ancestors decided to put all their knowledge into boxes—the Compartments of Knowledge. We became useless and unable to think or reason on our own.

GIRL: *(Stunned)* What else? What else changed in those days?

MAN:	One of our great strengths was our ability to use our brains. We could live by ourselves if we chose. We could live far away from the Compartments of Knowledge. We had wisdom. We could make decisions.
NARRATOR 2:	In those days the people were thinkers.
NARRATOR 1:	Yes. They had great knowledge and were able to share it with others in magical ways. The children went to large buildings where they were trained by older members of the group to think and reason and create. The older members could gather all the knowledge they wanted or discard some of it if they chose to. There was all kinds of thinking going on by the people.
GIRL:	(*Amazed*) I don't understand, were there different kinds of thinking?
WOMAN:	There were different kinds of things to learn. Also, people enjoyed sharing their ideas with each other, in a human sort of way.
BOY:	There must have been many changes. Is that right?
MAN:	Yes, but you must remember that the changes of which I speak took place over many generations. Perhaps one of the great changes was when our people began to live in larger and larger villages. These were villages of many houses, many buildings. This was the time when the village of which we our now part was built.
GIRL:	So, our village has not been here since the beginning of time?
WOMAN:	No, but our people are ancient people. We have been on this land for many, many years (*gesturing with her hands*). It is here, however, in this special place that we built a great village. It is here where our peoples have lived for many centuries. It is here where our peoples have built structures, erected dwellings, and tended to the land. It is here (*gesturing with her hands*) where our great and thriving population

settled and prospered. We raised tall towers and built great cities. We raised our children to be strong and proud. We placed our symbols on walls to celebrate our language and to celebrate our legends.

MAN: And that is why the decision of the Compartments of Knowledge is so difficult.

NARRATOR 2: *(Dryly)* The Compartments of Knowledge have decided that the people must go. They have decided that humans are no longer necessary. They have decided that humans are inconsequential.

GIRL: But we cannot leave! This is our home. This is where we live and where we have become one with every other person.

WOMAN: Is there no other way?

MAN: I'm afraid not. The Compartments of Knowledge have made their decision, and we must obey.

BOY: But I don't want to leave. Here is where I grew up. This is all I know. I do not want to leave.

MAN: I understand your concern. But we must listen to the wisdom of the Compartments of Knowledge. They are the ones who guide and lead our people.

WOMAN: *(Upset)* But this is not fair. We have been here for many years.

GIRL: *(Fearfully)* I am greatly saddened by this turn of events. How can we leave behind our customs and traditions? We were here long before the Compartments of Knowledge ever came into existence. *We* created *them*; they did not create us. We should be their masters, not the other way around.

BOY: Yes, can't anyone do anything for us?

MAN: We used to have much magic, but that is gone now. We have given all the magic to the Compartments of Knowledge.

GIRL:	Perhaps, if we could learn to think again.
WOMAN:	Maybe. But, that would take many centuries.
GIRL:	It might take a long time, but wouldn't it be worth it? Wouldn't it make a difference to all the generations that follow us?
WOMAN:	You might be right. Yes, what if we learned to think again?
NARRATOR 1:	The planet Earth has been home to humans for many thousands of years. Beginning in the middle of Africa and eventually spreading out to each of the seven continents, people learned how to use fire, construct large cities, employ language, invent machines, and explore the farthest reaches of the universe.
NARRATOR 2:	But they also invented the Compartments of Knowledge—devices that, over a span of many years, took on more and more of the thinking and deciding and creating. Now, a machine—a machine that never ages, never needs to be replaced, and never wears out—does the thinking.
NARRATOR 1:	But these humans still have the power—the power to change. Will they use it, or will it be forever lost? *(Pointing to audience)* What do you think?
NARRATOR 2:	*(Emphatically and pointing to audience)* Yes, *what . . . do . . . you . . . think?*

Possible Extensions

1. Invite students to create a readers theatre script about what would happen if computers took control of the world. How would life be different? What would change?

2. Ask students to search through library resources or Internet sites to locate information about the history of computers. What is considered the first computer? What can computers do today that they couldn't do five years ago?

3. What will be the state of computers in our society 100 years from now? 500 years from now? Will computers be an integral part of our everyday lives or just a necessary nuisance?

4. What basic human function would you like computers to do for you on a regular basis? Invite students to choose sides and debate the wisdom or practicality of computers taking over basic human endeavors.

 FOREVER IS A LONG TIME

Introduction

People have talked about immortality for a long time. The search for the "Fountain of Youth" has been a quest of many explorers. But there may be a price to pay for an extended life. This script poses some interesting questions for discussion and reflection.

Staging

The main character (Foster) is standing to the left of the staging area. The script begins with three news reporters standing in a small group to the right of Foster. As the story unfolds other reporters (4, 5, 6) walk onto the staging area, join the main group and ask their questions. The narrator is off to the side and in the background.

Narrator
X

Reporter 4
X

Reporter 1
X

Foster   Reporter 2   Reporter 5
X   X   X

Reporter 3
X

Reporter 6
X

NARRATOR: *(Calmly)* The scene takes place inside an old, dusty airplane hanger near a large East-coast city. The gathering of people inside the hanger is small and everyone is focused on the tall individual who calls himself "Foster." He has arrived at the hanger by himself. Just a few days previous he was undergoing extensive tests and diagnostic workups at one of the most prestigious hospitals in the world. Just prior to that, he had walked in off the street to a small office in Washington, D.C., and made a startling announcement. Everyone was amazed, and when the reports came back from the hospital confirming that what he said was absolutely true, the world found out, for the first time, who he really was.

As we begin, several carefully selected newspaper reporters surround the man. It is they who will release the news about this individual—a man whom nobody has seen before but whom everyone will get to know in a matter of hours.

REPORTER 1:   *(Very excited)* We just got the news, sir, and we're not quite sure what is going on. Could you please tell us?

FOSTER: *(Matter of factly)* Of course. It's very simple. I'm 648 years old.

REPORTER 2:   *(Skeptically)* That's sort of difficult to believe, sir. I mean anyone just looking at you would say that you are about 50 years old. You have a few wrinkles, a couple of gray hairs, and a receding hairline, but, at the most, you're only a middle-aged man.

FOSTER: I beg to differ with you. You see, I was born a long time ago. I have seen brave explorers cross the Atlantic Ocean looking for new lands and great riches. I have seen scientists discover new forms of life. I watched your United States begin its new life in what was then a small village known as Philadelphia. I saw the horrors of a civil war tear a country apart and pit brother against brother. I witnessed two great wars fought on the battlefields of Europe—wars in which enormous numbers of men, women, and children were killed. And I have seen the great discoveries made in space—new worlds and new frontiers. I have been here for it all—for more than 600 years.

REPORTER 3:	*(Amazed)* You realize, of course, that we all find this very difficult to believe. What makes you think that we're going to believe·anything you say?
FOSTER:	You must believe it. Some of the finest scientific minds in the world have examined me. They have carefully poked and probed my body with all their scientific instruments, monitors, and medical devices. They all, every one of them, have confirmed that my body is ageless. In fact, the great scientific minds have discovered that for every twelve of your years I only age one year. So, as far as I am concerned, I'm just 54 years old.
REPORTER 4:	Okay, let's get this straight. You're only 54 years old in your time—which is 648 years in our time. Is that right?
FOSTER:	That's right!
REPORTER 5:	*(Emphatically)* Okay, let's assume, for the time being, that all the scientists in the world are right, that you are really 648 years old, and that you have lived through all sorts of historical events and wars and kings and presidents and all of that. What I don't understand is how did this happen? What happened 648 years ago that caused your body to age only one year for every twelve of our years?
FOSTER:	Let's see if I can describe it. You see, I was born in a small mining village deep in the mountains. My family and every other family in that village were all miners. They had always been miners and had always spent their lives underground. Shortly before my birth, there was an unusual discovery in one of the mines. One of the miners discovered a small glowing rock; a rock that no one had ever seen before. The rock glowed brightly in the darkness of the mine, but when it was brought to the surface it looked just like ever other rock that had ever been mined.
REPORTER 6:	Did anyone know what kind of rock it was?

FOSTER: No, that was the strange part. Although everyone in the village, including their parents and their parents' parents had always been miners and had always known everything there was to know about rocks and minerals, nobody had ever seen a rock like that before. It was a new discovery.

REPORTER 1:   So, what was done with the rock?

FOSTER: My father was the oldest miner in the group, which meant that he was also the leader of all the miners. So he took the rock home and placed it on a small table in our hut. During the day it stayed there and looked just like every other rock. But at night, when my mother and father dimmed their candles, the rock glowed with a brilliance they had never seen before.

REPORTER 2:   *(With disbelief)* Okay, I guess I'm missing something. What does the rock have to do with the fact that you're more than 600 years old?

FOSTER: My mother was pregnant with me at the time and, quite naturally, she spent a lot of time in the hut while my father was deep inside the mines with all the other men. Nobody is sure, but we think that the glow from the rock somehow affected my mother's pregnancy. A few months later, I was born and looked just like every other baby in the village, but I was different somehow. My parents, who were very poor, didn't know what it was, but they noticed that I grew a little differently than the other children, I learned things a little differently, and, in a way, I looked different, too.

REPORTER 3:   What do you mean by "different"?

FOSTER: It wasn't that I was ugly or had any deformities that anyone could see. It was just that I was growing at a different rate than all the other kids in the village. I guess my parents were a little frightened for my safety, so they sent me to live with my grandmother in a village far away. You see, there were lots of superstitions in those days, and people didn't always understand when children were different. People often thought that the devil or some evil powers possessed those "different" children. So, my parents sent me away.

REPORTER 4: What happened then?

FOSTER: Well, I lived a life just like anyone else, except for the fact that I just wasn't getting any older—at least not getting older like the others in the village. I watched throughout the years as the people around me grew up, got old, and then died. Friends that I played with aged 12 times faster than I did, and they were old or dead by the time I was five or six years old. Everyone would point at me and say that I was a strange individual. Nobody could figure out why I wasn't getting old while everyone else was.

REPORTER 5: So, what did you do?

FOSTER: I had to move from one village to the next. I couldn't spend very much time in any single village. If I did, people would discover my secret. They would want to touch me, hoping that this "power" would somehow rub off on them. As soon as people noticed that I wasn't getting any older, they wanted to spend all their time with me. They wanted to be next to me. I couldn't go anywhere without crowds of people surrounding me hoping that my longevity would somehow affect them too.

REPORTER 6: How were you able to handle all that attention?

FOSTER: I didn't. I thought it would be better to just keep moving around. I figured if I didn't settle down for very long, then people wouldn't discover my little secret. I'd stay in some place for about 10 years or so, and then I would move on to a distant city or a faraway country. The good thing was that I was able to see a lot of the world and a lot of historical events. I knew I was aging very slowly, and I knew that I had lots of time on my hands, so I decided to really take my time going through life. I didn't know exactly how long I was going to live, but I did know that it was going to be a very very long time, so I figured that one of the best things I could do was to travel around the world and watch history in the making. Of course I never knew what was going to happen, but I did know that the world was constantly changing—that there would be wars, diseases, and discoveries. I wanted to keep my ears and eyes open and be ready to watch some of those things happen.

REPORTER 1:   *(Sarcastically)* So, you just went around the world waiting for history to happen?

FOSTER: Well, not exactly. You see, I couldn't stay in one place for very long simply because people would find out who I was or *what* I was. So, every 5 or 10 years, I would move to a different place, sometimes even a different country. I guess I've lucky because I have seen some of the world's most interesting historical events. The events that students read about in their history books are events that I saw with my own eyes.

REPORTER 2:   Tell us about some of those events.

FOSTER: I won't tell you about all of them because we don't have enough time, but I'll tell you about a few that had to do with the history of this country you now call the United States.

REPORTER 3:   In the United States, what, in your memory, was the most important historical event you witnessed?

FOSTER: It was when I traveled with Leif Eriksson. That was when he and his brave band of men set foot on what is now the United States. That was a difficult and long journey filled with many discoveries. To this day, I still can't understand why Leif and his men are not given credit for the original discovery of this land.

REPORTER 2:   What's another event in this country's history that you saw with your own eyes?

FOSTER: One year, I walked with some pioneers who were trying to cross the country on a wagon train. It was one of the most strenuous journeys of my life. There were diseases, long hours, harsh weather, and any number of troubles that we had to deal with. We started out with 131 people when we left Independence, Missouri, and ended up with only 78 when we reached the Oregon coast.

REPORTER 3:   Anything else that you remember?

FOSTER: I remember the American Civil War. That was a time when brother fought brother. It was a time when this country was divided and its citizens were fighting for its very survival. The events and circumstances that took place in the middle of the nineteenth century were some of the most profound in U.S. history.

REPORTER 6:   That's all well and good, but what happens now? You've been examined by some of the finest doctors in the world, and they all agree that you are 648 years old—the oldest human being who has ever lived—but what happens to you now? What will you do next? Where will you go?

FOSTER: That is a very good question and one I have thought about for a long time. Indeed, I have had a long time to think about it. After all these years, I have decided that it is time to die.

ALL REPORTERS: DIE?!

FOSTER: Yes, I have lived a long life. I have seen many things, met many people, and observed history in the making through-out the world. This should be the end of my time. I am cursed. I am cursed with near-immortality. I am cursed by a small glowing rock, discovered hundreds of years ago, that set me out on a path I never asked for, never wanted. I know it is a curse that will never go away, never leave me until the day I die.

REPORTER 5:   (*Amazed*) What are you talking about? Throughout the centuries, explorers have searched in vain for the Fountain of Youth, for the magic elixir that will preserve their lives and guarantee them eternal youth.

REPORTER 4:   Yes, that's right. Wars have been fought and enormous sums of money have been spent in order to find ways of preserving human life. Expeditions have set out across vast uncharted water looking for the answer, and science and medicine have devoted much time to discovering the secret of youth. You have it! And, now you want to end it?

FOSTER: Think of the consequences for me. I could live forever. I could live until the end of time. I could live until every single last star in the universe burns out and all that is left, the only thing remaining in that universe, is me. After every human being is gone, after every civilization is wiped out, after every known or unknown form of life that has ever existed or will ever exist is snuffed out, I will still be around. In short, ladies and gentlemen, I could end up being the last living thing in the universe. I would be alone, forever and ever and ever. That's not a fate I want. My life has been rich. My life has been complete. My life has been more full than anyone would ever think possible. What more can a person ask for? But now it is time to stop. Because if I don't stop it now, I will live forever and ever and ever.

NARRATOR: And with those words, the human being known as "Foster" turned and left the ancient airplane hanger. Everyone just stared as he walked to the far end of the tarmac. He kept walking, kept walking into the sunset that filtered through the clouds. No one stopped him. No one said anything. Everybody just stood there and watched as the oldest human being in the history of mankind walked out toward the horizon. He was gone . . . gone forever!

Possible Extensions

1. Invite students to discuss the concept of immortality. If they had a choice would they want to be immortal? What would be some of the benefits? What would be some of the drawbacks?

2. Invite students to discuss some of the scientific or medical advances/discoveries that are being made today. How are some of those discoveries helping people live longer lives? Are some of those discoveries contributing to our overall longevity?

3. Invite students to create a readers theatre script in which every individual has a choice of how long he or she gets to live. Each individual can make the choice only once in their lives, and when that choice is made, it can never be changed. Plan time to discuss the implications of those choices.

4. Students may be interested in reading the book *Tuck Everlasting* by Natalie Babbitt. Take time to discuss the parallels between that story and this script. How are they similar; how are they different?

JUST A THOUGHT

Introduction

Reading minds has been a parlor trick for many years, but what if there was a machine that really could read your subconscious thoughts? What would it reveal? Would you want to know? Would anyone else want to know, or is this a topic that is best left undiscovered?

Staging

The five characters may all be seated at a round or rectangular table. In the middle of the table is a small box (the shape and size do not matter). One character (Xyr) enters and exits the staging area periodically. The narrators are off to the side and can be standing on a podium or at a lectern.

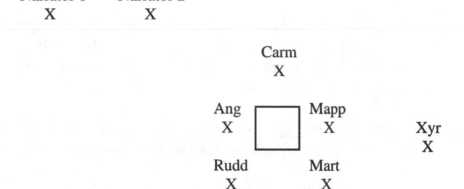

Narrator 1   Narrator 2
    X   X

                        Carm
                         X

              Ang ┌──────┐ Mapp
               X   │   │   X   Xyr
                   │   │   X
                   └──────┘
              Rudd   Mart
               X   X

NARRATOR 1:   In 2121, scientists created many new inventions and made many new discoveries. One of the most promising inventions was a device that could be used to read people's minds. This invention, known as the "Mind Mapper," was tested for many years, and after seemingly endless experimentation, it was distributed to a limited number of people on a trial basis. It was deemed safe by the scientists, but it had never been used outside the laboratory.

NARRATOR 2: In order to test its effectiveness, 100 Mind Mappers were distributed to selected individuals around the country. These individuals were chosen not because they were scientists but because they had been identified as clear and logical thinkers who could be trusted with this new technology. In order to be absolutely safe, each Mind Mapper was assigned a Monitor—a cyborg that was instructed to watch how each Mind Mapper was used, adjust any controls or dials, and intervene in the event of an emergency.

NARRATOR 1: As our play opens it's a Tuesday morning in Seattle. The sun is just beginning to creep up over the horizon. The day dawns clear and bright as a small band of seagulls glides through the air overhead. The sounds of traffic can be heard in the distance. The city is waking, wiping the slumber from its eyes, and rising to meet the day. Five people have gathered at the Sunrise Diner to share an early morning cup of coffee and some conversation.

XYR: *(Walking to the table; speaking with a robotic voice)* Here is the Mind Mapper. I will put it on the table. It is charged for one dose. You *(points to Carm)* may use it now. I will watch from over here.

CARM: *(Somewhat excited)* You know, ever since I was assigned one of these *(points to the Mind Mapper)* I've been anxious to use it.

ANG: *(With a sly smile)* What are you going to do with it, Carm? Whose mind do you want to read?

MART: It could be pretty interesting. We just have to be sure we pick the right person.

RUDD: *(Stands up and paces across staging area)* Well, I for one don't believe in these things *(points to the Mind Mapper)*. I just don't think that a machine with some wires and lights and other stuff that I don't understand could probe inside someone's mind and read what's in there. I don't think scientists are that smart yet. And what's with this cyborg? Why does this guy have to be hanging around? *(Sits down)*

CARM:	(*Calmly*) He's there to be sure that the Mind Mapper is used properly. He's not hurting anybody.
RUDD:	(*Scared*) I don't know. He's sort of creepy. I'm just uncomfortable when he's around.
MAPP:	Sounds like you've got something to hide, Rudd.
RUDD:	(*Stands up; speaks loudly*) I don't have anything to hide. Even if I did, I don't believe some silly little machine could look into my head and tell everyone what it is. This thing (*points to the Mind Mapper*) is just a bunch of junk, that's all. Just a bunch of junk!
XYR:	(*Robotically*) This is a scientific machine. Many scientists have tested it. It has been tested for many years. It is safe. It is safe to use to read people's minds. It is a machine that will probe the deepest recesses of the human mind. It will provide much information.
RUDD:	(*Sarcastically*) Yeah, right! And I'm the President of Bolivia!
ANG:	Rudd seems to be a little doubtful about the ability of this machine to read minds. Maybe he's afraid that we'll discover something inside his head that he doesn't want us to know about.
MAPP:	Or maybe we'll discover that there really isn't anything at all inside his head. What do you say to that, Rudd?
RUDD:	(*Stands up and paces around the table*) I think you're all a bunch of fools. First of all, I've got plenty in my head. I've got more there than the four of you put together. And, second, I'm just not convinced that anyone could invent a machine that can read minds. Yeah, there are machines that can travel faster than the speed of light. There are machines that can operate on humans without any doctors around. And there are machines that can mine precious minerals on distant planets. But a machine that can look inside someone's head and see what they're thinking—it's just not possible. (*Sits down*)

MART: (*Taunting*) I don't know. It still seems as though Rudd is trying to hide something from us. Or maybe he's just afraid of what we will discover. What do you say, Rudd?

CARM: Rudd, are you going to volunteer?

RUDD: (*Throwing up his hands*) Yeah, why not? Sure, I'll do it just to prove that you guys don't have any idea what you're talking about.

MAPP: I think we'd all be interested in knowing what's on Rudd's mind. What do you say?

RUDD: (*Impatiently*) I said I would do it, didn't I? I've got nothing to hide. So if you want to, go ahead and try it on me.

MART: I don't know, maybe he *does* have something to hide that he doesn't want us to know about. You know, you've been spending a lot of time by yourself lately, Rudd.

RUDD: So?

MART: Well, it's just that we haven't seen much of you lately. You've been in your garage a lot. And we know you don't have an old vehicle that you're refurbishing. And you don't have any hobbies or anything. I guess I'm just interested in what you are doing in there.

RUDD: (*Somewhat indignant*) What's that got to do with anything? I just like to spend some time in my garage, that's all. It's nothing; it's just something I like to do, that's all. Let's forget about that and get this mind reading stuff over with. I can't wait to show you guys up.

ANG: I can't wait to see what's going on inside your head.

CARM: Okay, here it goes. Are you ready, Rudd?

RUDD: Yeah, let's get it over with.

CARM:	(*He slides the box across the table so it is in front of Rudd*) Okay, now I'll turn it on just like they showed me in the training school.
NARRATOR 1:	There was complete silence. Everyone was looking at Rudd, who didn't move or say anything. Suddenly he slumped over in his chair.
ANG:	(*Frightened*) Hey, what happened? What's happened to Rudd? Look at him . . . he's just lying there, slumped over in his chair not doing anything. What's happening? What's happening?
XYR:	(*Robotically*) You are not to worry. Your friend is safe. Nothing will happen to him. He is okay. His mind has just been read by the Mind Mapper. It is perfectly safe. He is not in danger. His mind must now recover. Do not worry about him. He is perfectly safe.
CARM:	(*Fearfully*) Did I do something wrong? He doesn't look good. Did I do something wrong?
XYR:	Nothing is wrong. He is fine. Look at the box now.
MAPP:	Hey, look. The cyborg's right. Look at the box.
MART:	(*Excitedly*) Yeah, look! Can you see it? Can you see what the dials are doing? Look at them!
CARM:	(*Looking at the box and extremely excited*) Oh my gosh. I can't believe what I'm seeing. Look, guys!
ANG:	(*Looking at the box; extremely excited*) Oh my word! This is simply incrediblc. I just can't believe it. Wow, this is un-believable! (*Stands up*)
MAPP:	(*Excitedly and looking at the box*) Wow! And I mean WOW! Who would have thought? I just can't believe it.
MART:	(*Looks at the box and stands up*) This I cannot believe. It's really scary. It's really scary and unbelievable (*points at the box*). What do we do now?

XYR: You only have one look. There is only one charge on the box. You wanted to look. Now, you cannot look any more. You must take what you saw. There is no more to see. You must deal with what you saw. That is all now. I will take the box. I will go. *(Xyr departs)*

NARRATOR 2:   And so the cyborg, Xyr, picked up the box and left. The group was silent for a long time. Still slumped over in his chair was their companion Rudd. It would be only a matter of minutes before he would regain consciousness, before he would be fully awake and active, and then the group would have to deal with what they had seen. They would have to deal with the fact that their companion—a person they had known for many years—had a thought in his head that was more terrible than any they could ever conceive.

NARRATOR 2:   It was the most horrible thought of all, a thought that would affect each of them, a thought that would forever change their lives. It was the worst of the worst, and they only had a few moments to decide what they would do about it. Just a few moments to make a decision that would forever seal their fate.

NARRATOR 1:   *(Pointing to the audience; speaking in a foreboding voice)* And so, we ask you—what was that thought? What was the horrible thought that filled Rudd's head? You only have a few minutes. Make your decision now, before it's too late!

Possible Extensions

1. Divide the class into several small groups and invite each group to decide on the most terrible thought of all. What do they think Rudd's thought was? What made it so horrible?

2. Invite students to craft an extension to this script—an extension that shares the terrible thought discovered in Rudd's mind and how the members of the group dealt with that thought.

3. Invite students to discuss and comment on the ability to read people's minds. Do they think it will be possible to do that in the future? Would they want to have that power? What would they do with that power?

PART V

Future World

A LONG, LONG TIME

Introduction

What if there was truly a "utopia?" Would you go? You only have a few minutes to make your decision—a decision that is irreversible. Quickly now, what would you do?

Staging

The five characters can be seated at a round or rectangular table. If a table is unavailable, place five chairs in a circle. The new student (Bob) enters the staging area about halfway through the production but does not sit down. The narrator is off to the side and can be standing on a podium or at a lectern.

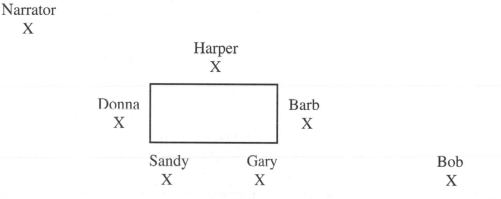

NARRATOR:	The time is the present in a small town somewhere in Arizona. It is a sunny Thursday afternoon, and the students at Midvale High School have just gotten out of school. Some have gone off to jobs, others have gone home, and a few are hanging around the local fast food place making plans for the weekend.
HARPER:	*(In a bored voice)* Man, I just don't know what to do this weekend. It's so dead in this town. There aren't any good movies playing, and the football team's playing an away game, so that's out. It just looks like it's going to be another dead weekend . . . AGAIN!

DONNA:	*(Bored and tired)* Yeah, it's just sooooo dead in this town. Nothing ever happens. I mean, it's really boring!
SANDY:	*(Somewhat excited; stands up)* Hey, did anyone see that flash of light last night. I was outside in the backyard with my little sister, and there was this streak of light that flashed over the mountains to the south *(points)*.
BARB:	You think it was some kind of shooting star or something?
SANDY:	I don't know. I've never seen one before. What do they look like?
GARY:	I think they look just like one of those planes from out at the Air Force base. You know, when they zoom overhead at high altitudes they leave a trail of smoke in the sky. Maybe your shooting star was one of those air force planes testing something.
SANDY:	I don't know. It sure seemed strange. Did anyone else see it?
ALL:	*(Shaking their heads and murmuring)* No, not me.
SANDY:	It was weird. One minute it appeared overhead, and then it just seemed to fall from the sky and land on the ground.
BARB:	*(Quickly changing the subject)* Hey, girls, anyone see that new guy who checked into school this morning. *(Excitedly)* I mean, was he good lookin' or what?
HARPER:	Is that all you girls look for—whether a guy is good looking or not? How 'bout someone with some personality.
DONNA:	*(Sarcastically)* The next time you get some personality, Harper, please let us all know, and we'll be sure to come beat down your door.
BARB:	He sure was cute. I think he was assigned to Mr. Creeper's homeroom. I saw him in algebra class this morning. He didn't say anything. He just sort of stared straight ahead for most of the time. He's good looking, but he seemed odd.

SANDY:	I don't know, but we could sure use a little excitement around here. It's going to be another dull weekend. I wouldn't mind a date with some new, good-looking guy.
GARY:	*(Sarcastically)* You wouldn't mind a date with some creature from the black lagoon!
SANDY:	*(In a mock threat)* Hey, how would you like me to take this fist and . . .

The new kid interrupts by slowly walking over to the group and standing beside them. He doesn't smile, and he doesn't say anything. The girls in the group are dazzled and amazed. The boys in the group are suspicious and wary.

HARPER:	Hey, you're the new kid aren't you? Where are you from? What's your name?
BOB:	*(Slowly, deliberately, and mysteriously)* Oh, I just got in last night. I came from far away . . . from a place that is far, far away. It was a long trip . . . a very long trip. I'm part of a large group, I mean, family. We'll only be here for a short time, and then we must leave.
GARY:	I don't get it. How come you're only going to be here for a short time?
BOB:	*(Slowly and deliberately)* That's just the way it is. I can only stay for a little while, and then I must go.
GARY:	*(Skeptically)* Oh.
SANDY:	You look like you've played some football. Are you thinking about trying out for the team?
BOB:	*(Looking at each of the others very slowly, one at a time.)* I don't know football. Besides, I have other things to do.
SANDY:	*(Cautiously)* Oh.
HARPER:	So, what is your name?

BOB:	*(Mysteriously)* My name does not mean anything, but I guess you could call me Bob.
HARPER:	Okay, Bob, what do you do? It's obvious that you don't play football, you're from some place far away, you're new here in town, and all the girls here *(he sweeps his hand)* think you're really cute.
ALL GIRLS:	*(Indignantly)* Heeeeeeeey!!!
HARPER:	So, what is it? Who are you?
BOB:	*(Again, looking slowly and deliberately at each person in the circle.)* I'm what you would call a transporter.
GARY:	*(Slightly confused)* A transporter! What the heck is that?
BOB:	I take people to a happy place. I take people to a place that is far away . . . a place that is beyond this world and in another dimension. A place of great happiness and great joy. A place filled with activities beyond your imagination. It is a place your scholars have called Nirvana.
GARY:	*(Sarcastically)* Yeah, right buddy. And I'm the president of the United States and have about 6 trillion dollars in my bank account right now.
BOB:	*(Staring at Gary—expressionless)* Well, what if I could promise you great happiness . . . great happiness for the rest of your life? You would never be bored, never angry, and never sad. Every day would be a good day.
DONNA:	*(Sarcastically)* So, you're the tooth fairy, right?
BOB:	*(Turning and staring at her mysteriously)* No, I'm just a simple transporter. I can take you to the place of joy.
BARB:	So, how do you take us to this great place of happiness. *(Chuckling)* Do you have some sort of spaceship, some sort of magic beam that shoots us up into space?

BOB:	No, I simply have these. *(He pulls five small objects from his pocket [grapes are suggested] and places them on the table.)*
SANDY:	There are five of those things and five of us.
GARY:	*(Sarcastically)* Brilliant observation, Sherlock!
HARPER:	So, what do these things here do?
BOB:	I'm not permitted to tell you. All I can say is that I had my first one a long, long time ago.
DONNA:	What do you mean, a long, long time ago?
BOB:	*(Looking carefully and slowly around the group)* In your Earth years, I took my first one more than 7,693 years ago.
BARB:	*(Amazed)* You mean . . . I mean . . . you mean you're . . .
SANDY:	*(Equally astounded)* You can't be. You're just like us. You're not more than 17, 18 years old.
BOB:	What you see on the outside of me is just my Earth form. On the inside of me is my real form. Let me show you. *(He moves so his back is to the audience and pretends to open his shirt to the other players.)*
ALL GIRLS:	*(Screaming)* No, No, No!
ALL BOYS:	*(Yelling)* You've got to be kidding!
SANDY:	*(Amazed)* Then, it *is* true! You are . . . I mean . . . You are who you say you are.
GARY:	And, what you're saying is that we can live to be really old just by eating one of these things here?
BOB:	*(With a Cheshire grin)* Oh, yes. You will experience eternal bliss, and you will live a long time. You'll get the two things you have most wanted in life just by eating this one item. So, what do you say?

HARPER:	*(Suspicious)* I'm not so sure.
BARB:	*(Softly)* I'm not so sure either.
GARY:	*(Boldly)* Hey, anybody game? I mean, what can it hurt? Things are pretty dull around here anyway. A guarantee of happiness and a long life can't be all that bad.
SANDY:	*(Cautiously)* I'm not so sure.
DONNA:	Well, I'm game. What the heck. It's going to be another dull weekend in this loser town anyway. I say we bring a little excitement into our lives. I'm goin' for it! *(She reaches over, picks up one of the objects [a grape] on the table and puts it in her mouth.)*
BOB:	*(With a big smile on his face)* You are wise, my chosen one.
DONNA:	*(Smiling, but in a trance)* I . . . will . . . go . . . with . . . you . . . now.
BOB:	*(Touching her lightly on the shoulder)* Come with me now.

Bob and Donna slowly exit while the others stare at them, mouths agape.

NARRATOR:	And so it was, in a small town in Arizona, when a stranger came to visit. He brought with him the offer of great happiness and a long life. He brought the people of the town a way out of their unhappiness. He brought them hope. He brought them dreams. He brought them a promise of what could be. But, he also brought them something else . . . something they never bargained for. He made wishes come true—but, as always in life, there was a price to pay.

Possible Extensions

1. Invite students to discuss what eternal happiness means to them. If they could have it, would they want it?

2. Invite the class to discuss the four remaining objects on the table. Will the other members of the group eat those objects or will they leave them there? Which members of the group are most likely to eat the items?

3. Invite students to create a readers theatre script that extends this one. What will the four remaining members of the group do? What will happen to Donna and Bob?

4. Invite students to discuss the scientific reality of long lives. What type of research is being done to extend the lives of human beings? How old is the oldest person in the world? What can people do (diet, exercise, etc.) to prolong and extend their lives?

INTO, BEYOND, AND BACK AGAIN

Introduction

Traveling from one place to another takes time. What if it was possible to begin and end a trip in a matter of microseconds? What if it involved a major change—a change in you? Would you be willing?

Staging

Each of the characters slowly walks to the front of the staging area and speaks directly to the audience. Each character speaks in a dull, dry monotone—completely lacking any emotion. After this individual presentation, each character walks to the front left portion of the staging area and turns his or her back to the audience. There is a table in the middle of the staging area. On the table should be a fax machine, portable photocopy machine, or some similar device. The narrators can be placed on a podium or at a lectern at the front right portion of the staging area.

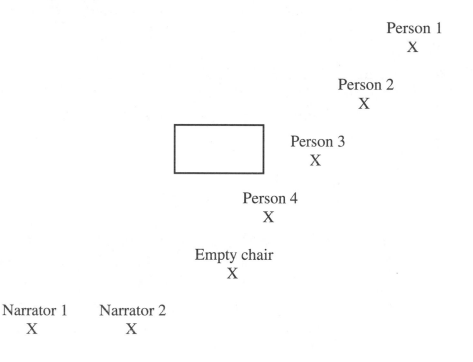

125

NARRATOR 1:   It is the middle of the twenty-fourth century. Great scientific discoveries have been made. In recent years, new advances in travel have been examined and explored. In the past, humans were dependent on vehicles to get from place to place. But all of those vehicles needed power and energy, and in the middle of the twenty-fourth century power and energy are extremely limited.

NARRATOR 2:   A small group of scientists have been working on a form of travel that does not rely on specialized forms of power. They have been studying molecular travel. That is, the ability to reduce a person to his or her individual molecules, stream those molecules over vast distances (between galaxies, for example) and reconfigure them into the humans they were at the beginning. The advantages of this form of travel are obvious. Little power is necessary, and enormous distances can be covered in mere seconds.

NARRATOR 1:   And so, in a secret location high in the Sangre de Cristo Mountains of New Mexico a small band of scientists and an intrepid group of volunteers have just completed the first, highly secret human experiments in molecular travel. Let's hear their stories.

PERSON 1:   *(Robotically)* I was one of the first volunteers to come to this place. I read about this venture and decided to make the journey from my home planet of Altair VI. After I arrived, I was escorted to a secret location. The next day I met the other members of my troop. We were excited about the possibilities; we just didn't know the consequences. *(Walks away and turns his/her back)*

NARRATOR 2:   The troop was composed of five members. None of them had any family members (that was a condition of the experiment). None had any special ties to their local community. Indeed, although it was never said, these individuals were chosen because if any of them disappeared, no one would notice.

PERSON 2: *(Without emotion)* I volunteered for this experiment because I was alone. I lived in Hawaii in the town of Makawao on Maui. Out of 24,295,973 applications mine was one of five chosen. After a series of seven interviews, the scientists selected me. I wanted to do something that would benefit everyone—not just the people here on Earth, but all the individuals and creatures throughout the universe, throughout the galaxy. *(Walks away and turns his/her back)*

NARRATOR 1: On the third day of their stay, the volunteers were led into a small, gray room on the outskirts of the facility. There is nothing in the room except for the Molecular Transporter *(points to the fax machine)* and a chair. Each volunteer was led to the chair and told to sit down. Each volunteer was told to put his or her left hand on the top of the molecular transporter and remain calm. *(In a mysterious voice)* All lights in the room were turned off and the transporter was switched on. There was no sound or light or motion. But slowly, very slowly, something began to change.

PERSON 3: I'll never forget sitting in that chair and putting my hand on top of the molecular transporter. It really was scary. And then it happened. Before I knew it, I was gone. I could see myself disappearing right before my eyes. In a matter of a minute I had been reduced to nothing more than a collection of molecules speeding through space. I was no longer an individual . . . just a bunch of flashing molecules.

NARRATOR 2: The scientists knew that their technology wasn't perfect. They just couldn't anticipate every contingency or every possibility. They believed that they had developed the transport of molecules over great distances, the reconstruction of those molecules into their original life-forms, and the reversal of that whole process in order to return the individual back to the original location. Prior to the human trials, the technology had been tested on a wide variety of lower life-forms—flowers, trees, fish, and small rodents—all with remarkable success.

NARRATOR 1:   But they couldn't know how effective their ideas were until they were tried out on the highest life-form—humans. They felt confident that the experiments with humans would be as successful as those with the lower life-forms. All their data pointed to that potential for success. They had factored in everything. Everything except . . .

PERSON 4:   *(Slowly and without emotion)* I, too, shall never forget sitting in that chair, putting my hand on the machine, and having my molecules sifted into a stream that sped out across the vast reaches of space. In seconds, my molecules reconfigured themselves into my whole self. And then, before I could think or breathe, I was streaming back across the solar system and to this place. I had absolutely no control over my body and no control over where I was going, and I came back different than when I left. I was forever changed.

NARRATOR 2:   The transport system worked beautifully. However, as our previous speaker *(points to Person 4)* shared with you, something did change. The scientists had perfected the material transport of molecules across vast distances, and they had perfected the mechanics necessary to reverse the process so that the individuals could return to their place of origin. But, they forgot one element. It was an element that, when missing, made all the difference . . . yes, it made all the diff . . .

PERSON 5:   *(Interrupting)* I, too, went from here to there and back again. But, like my comrades, I was different. I was the same on the outside, and I was the same on the inside. But, still, I had changed.

NARRATOR 1:   Yes, the experiment was a success—sort of. The scientists were able to transport higher life-forms across the reaches of space in the wink of an eye, but something was missing. You see, although their bodies could be conveyed through the vastness of space, their emotions could not.

NARRATOR 2:   The individuals before you are physically the same today as they were when they initially applied for this great experiment. They are the same, except, well . . .they're really different. As you probably noticed, their bodies look fine, but they have no emotions or feelings on the inside. Their bodies were transported, but when their molecules were broken down, their emotions had nothing in which to reside.

NARRATOR 1:   Their emotions, because they were not physical items, could not be transported, and so they vaporized. What you see before you *(sweeps hand across the actors on the staging area)* are the same individuals you would have seen several months ago, before the experiment began.

The actors turn around to face the audience, each with a blank stare.

NARRATOR 2:   But, look closely *(slowly pointing to each one)*. They *are not* the same as when they left. They are without feelings. They are without emotions. So, I guess, the larger question is this: Was the experiment truly a success, or did it leave something very essential behind? In other words, did these volunteers pay the greatest price of all? Did we gain, or did *they* lose?

Possible Extensions

1. Invite students to discuss the legal, ethical, or social implications of molecular transportation. What should scientists take into consideration if and when this technology becomes available?

2. Invite students to discuss the possible advantages of molecular transportation. How could it add to our knowledge of the distant reaches of space? How might it solve the problems here on Earth—particularly at this particular time in history?

3. If students could be instantly transported to one (and only one) location in the universe, where would they want to go? Invite students to share and discuss their choices. Is there any place that is more popular than others?

THE LAST DECISION

Introduction

Earth is dying and an important decision must be made. Who will go to a distant world to begin a new colony? The choice must be made quickly . . . there is no time to waste. Who do you choose?

Staging

There are two sets of five characters each. One set of characters does all of the speaking. They are grouped in a small circle on the right side of the staging area. The second set of characters is seated on chairs to the left of the staging area. They have no speaking parts. Four of them (scientist, politician, farmer, carpenter) should each be designated by a clearly marked sign. The fifth individual in the second group has no designation. The narrators can be positioned at a lectern or on a podium to the right of the staging area. There is an offstage voice throughout the presentation.

Sarah		scientist	
X		X	
Lynn Thomas		politician farmer	
X X		X X	
Serge		carpenter _____	
X		X X	
Narrator 1 Narrator 2			
X X			
			Offstage voice
			X

131

NARRATOR 1:   It is sometime in the future. An enormous meteor has been speeding toward Earth for several weeks. It has been calculated that it will crash into Earth with such force that the Earth will be knocked out of its orbit and sent spiraling toward the sun. Every nation and every country is in a panic. The meteor will strike Earth in less the three weeks.

NARRATOR 2:   In a secret location just outside the town of Durango, Colorado, a group of people have gathered. They are there to make one of the most important decisions in the history of mankind. Because of the impending danger from the meteor, a previously secret mission to colonize the moon has been put on the fast track. The rocket has limited space, and it must carry enough materials and food to help the colonists survive for an extended period of time.

NARRATOR 1:   Scientific instruments of every shape and size also need to be loaded aboard the spacecraft. Because there is not much room, which individuals will go to establish the new colony must be carefully considered. These individuals will be the only survivors of this cataclysmic event—the last human beings in the universe. Everyone else will be dead.

NARRATOR 2:   The group of people before you (*points to group of people on the left side of the staging area*) must decide on the last individual to go on this journey. Nine people are already standing by, ready to be loaded on the spacecraft. The final person to leave Earth must be chosen within the next five minutes. Who will be the final person to travel to the moon colony and, hopefully, establish a new civilization?

OFFSTAGE VOICE: (*Authoritatively*) Five minutes remaining for The Final Decision!

SARAH: (*Walking around*) Look at them there (*points to the group on the right side of the staging area*). They look scared. They *must* be scared. One of them will go. The others will have to stay.

LYNN: I guess we're the fortunate ones. We have already been chosen to go on the spacecraft to the new colony. But just think, everything we have known will be gone in an instant. By this time next month Earth will no longer exist. We will still be living, but nothing—*(frightened)* and I mean *nothing*—will live ever again on the planet Earth.

THOMAS: *(Frantic and shuffling across the staging area)* Just think, out of the millions and millions of people on Earth, we were the ones chosen to go. Wow, just think about it—we will live and millions and millions of people all over the world will be gone . . . POOF! . . . gone. Burned up . . . incinerated . . . vaporized . . . *gone*!

SERGE: Wow, it's incredible—we go, they die. But perhaps we shouldn't dwell on that because now we have to make the most important decision related to the fate of all human-kind. Which one of those people should we take with us? We don't have much time, but I'll tell you one thing, I'm really scared. What if we make a big mistake? There's no going back. What we choose is what we get.

OFFSTAGE VOICE: *(Authoritatively)* Four minutes remaining for The Final Decision!

SARAH: *(With assurance)* You know what I'm thinking? I'm thinking that we should take the scientist *(points to the scientist)*. After all, we'll need someone in the new colony who can help us invent new machines and new devices, so we can survive. Besides, a scientist is important in case there are any diseases or things that might infect us.

LYNN: I think Sarah has a good point. A scientist would be good to have in the new colony. But you know what? I think a politician should go along on this journey *(points to the politician)*. What is really going to help our colony survive is a government—one that is based on firm laws and established rules. Bringing a politician along would help us establish a free and democratic colony—one in which everyone is equal, and we all work together for the common good.

THOMAS:	*(Standing)* You make a good argument, Lynn, but I'm just not convinced that a politician is necessary. After all, we're intelligent people, and we can make our own decisions and our own laws. I'm just not sure that a politician would add anything to our small colony.
LYNN:	Well, then, who would your vote be for?
THOMAS:	*(Walking around)* I really think we should take the farmer along. After all, we do have to eat, and I think a farmer *(points to the farmer)* would be able to provide us with the food we need and would know the ways in which we need to grow and harvest that food. Without food or the means to grow that food, we will never survive. That's why I think the farmer is the most important person we can take along on this journey.
OFFSTAGE VOICE:	*(Authoritative)* Three minutes remaining for The Final Decision!
SERGE:	*(Unsure)* You make some good points, but I just don't know. Like Thomas said, we are all pretty intelligent, and I think we could figure out some ways to grow a bunch of food. I mean, my grandmother used to have a garden. I watched what she did, and I think I can figure out how to grow some corn or beans or spinach.
THOMAS:	*(Loudly)* Spinach? Yuck!
LYNN:	Hey guys, we have to decide pretty soon. What do you think, Serge?
SERGE:	*(Strongly)* My vote is for the carpenter *(points to the carpenter)*. Just think, without a carpenter we'll never be able to build anything. We'll have to build a hospital, a store, a power plant, and other important buildings. Without a carpenter, how are all those buildings going to come about? They've got to be built by someone, and that's why I think the carpenter is the best person to take along as part of our new colony.

OFFSTAGE VOICE: *(Authoritatively)* Two minutes remaining for The Final Decision!

SARAH: *(Hesitantly)* I just don't know. There's so much to think about, and we just don't have the time to think about it all. My vote still goes to the scientist. The scientist is a problem-solver by trade and can help us tackle any problem we might have. I still think that the best person to bring is the scientist!

LYNN: *(Standing and pointing)* My vote stays with the politician. Without a form of government, we will be doomed. The politician can help us get started right and can ensure that we have rules and laws that apply to everyone. Without those laws, we would be doomed my friends!

THOMAS: I'm sticking with the farmer *(points)*. I don't know about you guys, but I like to eat. If we can't get any food, then there is no way that we will survive for more than a few days or a few weeks. The farmer is the only one who can ensure that we will get that food and that we will survive.

OFFSTAGE VOICE: *(Authoritatively)* One minute remaining for The Final Decision!

SERGE: For me, there's only one choice: the carpenter. We need those hospitals, schools, stores, and other structures that are necessary in a new colony. We need the carpenter.

SARAH: *(Urgently)* Hey, guys, we're running out of time. We've got to decide now!

OFFSTAGE VOICE: *(Authoritatively)* Forty-five seconds remaining for The Final Decision!

LYNN: *(Quickly)* There's not enough time. What should we do?

THOMAS: *(Franticly)* Come on guys, let's decide now. Let's make our choice.

OFFSTAGE VOICE: *(Authoritatively)* Thirty seconds remaining for The Final Decision.

SERGE: *(In a panic, pacing quickly)* We need more time! We just don't have enough time. Oh my gosh, we've got to decide now! We've got to choose!

SARAH: *(Rapidly)* Quick, let's decide!

LYNN: *(Extremely anxious)* Who will it be?

THOMAS: *(Unsure)* Uhhh. Uhhh. I think it should be . . .

OFFSTAGE VOICE: *(Authoritatively)* Fifteen seconds remaining for The Final Decision!

SERGE: *(Loudly and with enthusiasm)* Look! *(Points to the anonymous individual in the fifth chair.)* What about that person? That person would be perfect.

SARAH: *(Excited)* Serge is right.

LYNN: *(Loudly)* Wow! Great!

THOMAS: *(With animated enthusiasm)* That's it! That's the one!

NARRATOR 1: And so it was that a mere three seconds before their time ran out, the group made its decision on the last individual to be taken to the new colony on the moon. Their choice proved to be the best one they could make. The tenth person was the ideal complement to the others.

NARRATOR 2: And so it was that the spacecraft blasted off from the secret launch site in southwestern Colorado and headed for the surface of the moon. Weeks later, in a cataclysmic explosion, the Earth was disintegrated. But the new colony had been established . . . and it thrived . . . thanks to that all-important decision made just in the nick of time.

NARRATOR 1:   And so I ask you *(points to audience)*, who was that final individual? What was the occupation or special skill that the individual had that ensured the success of the new colony? Who should have been the tenth individual on the journey?

NARRATOR 2:   Make your decision . . . time is running out!

Possible Extensions

1. Divide students into several small groups. Invite each group to come up with a list of 10 individuals they think should form the nucleus of a new colony on the surface of the moon. What jobs or occupations should the people have that would ensure the success of the colony?

2. Meteors have slammed into the Earth before. In fact, one theory attributes the elimination of dinosaurs to a meteor impact millions of years ago. Invite students to research "popular" meteor impacts (e.g., Meteor Crater in Arizona) and create a time line of those events.

DO IT YOURSELF!

Introduction

There are no characters in this script. The students all play themselves. Invite the selected actors to pencil in their names on the appropriate blanks below. In addition, there are several blanks inserted throughout the script. Students may complete these as part of an initial writing activity or on the spot as the script is being read. This script is designed to offer students opportunities to use their own imaginations and create their own science fiction readers theatre script. There are no right or wrong responses. In fact, this script can be done several different times by several different actors/writers, and each rendition will be different from every other presentation.

Staging

There is no narrator for this script. Students may be seated on chairs (as they would be in a classroom setting) or milling around (as they would be on the playground or at a mall).

1:_____   2:_____
         X   X

3:_____   4:_____
       X   X

     5:_____   6:_____
            X   X

1:   Hey, guys. I've got a great idea! We've been doing all those scripts in the *Science Fiction Readers Theatre* book our teacher has, but you know what? I think the author could have written some other stories.

2:   I think you're right. There are lots of different ways to look at science fiction.

139

3:   Exactly! Science fiction has no limits—it has no boundaries. I'm sure the author could have written a thousand different scripts.

4:   Yeah, you're right! Science fiction really taps into a person's creative spirit and shows that there is no limit to the imagination.

5:   Remember what our teacher said, "Science fiction is an imaginative story that is based either totally or partially on scientific facts or principles."

6:   I guess that leaves everything open to interpretation.

1:   You're right about that. You know, we could even draft some science fiction stories right here, on the spot, that could be used as possible readers theatre scripts.

2:   Hey, that sounds pretty neat. Why don't we try it?

3:   Okay, we could do one about the _____
_____
_____
_____
_____.

4:   Or maybe a story about when the whole country _____
_____
_____
_____
_____.

5:   And maybe one about when the school _____
_____
_____
_____
_____.

6: A story I'd like to do is one about _____
_____
_____
_____
_____.

1: That's just like the story about _____
_____
_____
_____
_____.

2: Boy, it sounds like we could come up with lots of science fiction scenarios.

3: You're right. In fact, we could develop science fiction scripts about things that happened in the past. For example, what if _____
_____
_____
_____?

4: Hey, that's nothing. What about _____
_____
_____
_____?

5: Think about this. What if _____
_____
_____
_____?

6: You know what would have been really strange? If _____
_____
_____
_____
_____.

1:   I know one thing—I wouldn't have wanted to _____.
Can you imagine _____

_____

_____

_____

_____?

2:   Not me! What about all those people who _____

_____

_____

_____

_____?

3:   But you know what? Science fiction can also take place in
the present. For example, just imagine if _____

_____

_____

_____

_____.

4:   Wow, that's neat. But what if _____

_____

_____

_____

_____?

5:   I sure wouldn't want to _____

_____

_____

_____

_____.

6:   Hey, don't forget one of the greatest science fiction topics—
computers! Just think if all the computers in the world

_____

_____

_____

_____

_____.

1: Yeah, computers could even _____

_____

_____

_____

_____.

2: What about some science fiction stories that could take place in the future. After all, the future is the unknown, and the future is still full of creativity, imagination, and an untold number of possibilities. What do you guys think? What kind of science fiction stories could we create for future events?

3: I think that _____

_____

_____

_____

_____.

4: I think a neat story could be one about _____

_____

_____

_____

_____.

5: How about one about _____

_____

_____

_____

_____?

6: Yeah, okay. But what about one that deals with _____

_____

_____

_____

_____?

1:   Or we could do one about _____

_____

_____

_____

_____.

2:   You know what? I think a great story would be one about

_____

_____

_____

_____.

3:   Hey! What kinds of stories will kids 100 years from now be writing?

4:   What about kids 500 years from now?

5:   What about kids 1,000 years from now?

6:   I don't know about you guys, but I think there's an awful lot of science fiction stories we could create. If we turned our stories into readers theatre scripts, we could share them with other classes. We could even videotape them and donate the tapes to the school library. Hey, maybe we could even send them to Hollywood. You never know when some talent scout or movie producer might be looking for a fresh, new script for the next summer blockbuster!

Possible Extensions

1. Invite students to complete the blanks and perform the script for another class. Encourage the two classes to engage in an active dialogue about their interpretations.

2. Encourage students to provide a copy of this script to several adults. Students should invite the adults to fill in the appropriate blanks on the script. Students can then perform the readers theatre script and discuss the adult's ideas.

3. Invite students to videotape their performance of this script. Place the videotape in the school library or community library.

Books About Readers Theatre

Braun, W., and C. Braun. *Readers Theatre: Scripted Rhymes and Rhythms*. Calgary, AB, Canada: Braun and Braun Educational Enterprises, 1995.

Coger, L. I., and M. R. White. *Readers Theatre Handbook: A Dramatic Approach to Literature*. Glenview, IL: Scott, Foresman, 1982.

Dixon, N., A. Davies, and C. Politano. *Learning with Readers Theatre: Building Connections*. Winnipeg, MB, Canada: Peguis, 1996.

Hill, S. *Readers Theatre: Performing the Text*. Armadale, Australia: Eleanor Curtain, 1990.

Johnson, T. D., and D. R. Louis. *Bringing It All Together: A Program for Literacy*. Portsmouth, NH: Heinemann, 1990.

Plant, R. *Readers Theatre in the Elementary Classroom: A Take Part Teacher's Guide*. North Vancouver, BC, Canada: Take Part Productions, 1990.

Shepard, A. *Stories on Stage: Scripts for Reader's Theater*. New York: H. W. Wilson, 1993.

Sloyer, S. *Readers Theatre: Story Dramatization in the Classroom*. Urbana, IL: National Council for Teachers of English, 1982.

Tanner, F. *Creative Communication: Projects in Acting, Speaking, Oral Reading*. Pocatello, ID: Clark, 1979.

———. *Readers Theatre Fundamentals*. Pocatello, ID: Clark, 1993.

Sources For Additional Readers Theatre Scripts

Barchers, S. *Fifty Fabulous Fables: Beginning Readers Theatre*. Englewood, CO: Teacher Ideas Press, 1997.

———. *From Atalanta to Zeus: Readers Theatre from Greek Mythology*. Englewood, CO: Teacher Ideas Press, 2001.

———. *Muticultural Folktales: Readers Theatre for Elementary Students*. Englewood, CO: Teacher Ideas Press, 2000.

———. *Readers Theatre for Beginning Readers*. Englewood, CO: Teacher Ideas Press, 1993.

———. *Scary Readers Theatre*. Englewood, CO: Teachers Ideas Press, 1994.

Criscoe, B. L., and P. J. Lanasa. *Fairy Tales for Two Readers*. Englewood, CO: Teacher Ideas Press, 1995.

Fredericks, A. D. *Frantic Frogs and Other Frankly Fractured Folktales for Readers Theatre*. Englewood, CO: Teacher Ideas Press, 1993.

————. *Readers Theatre for American History*. Englewood, CO: Teacher Ideas Press, 2001.

————. *Silly Salamanders and Other Slightly Stupid Stories for Readers Theatre*. Englewood, CO: Teacher Ideas Press, 2000.

————. *Tadpole Tales and Other Totally Terrific Treats for Readers Theatre*. Englewood, CO: Teacher Ideas Press, 1997.

Georges, C., and C. Cornett. *Reader's Theatre*. Buffalo, NY: D.O.K. Publishers, 1990.

Haven, K. *Great Moments in Science: Experiments and Readers Theatre*. Englewood, CO: Teacher Ideas Press, 1996.

Latrobe, K. H., C. Casey, and L. A. Gann. *Social Studies Readers Theatre for Young Adults*. Englewood, CO: Teacher Ideas Press, 1991.

Latrobe, K. H., and M. K. Laughlin. *Readers Theatre for Young Adults*. Englewood, CO: Teacher Ideas Press, 1989.

Laughlin, M. K., and K. H. Latrobe. *Readers Theatre for Children*. Englewood, CO: Teacher Ideas Press, 1990.

Laughlin, M. K., P. T. Black, and K. H. Latrobe. *Social Studies Readers Theatre for Children*. Englewood, CO: Teacher Ideas Press, 1991.

Pfeffinger, C. R. *Holiday Readers Theatre*. Englewood, CO: Teacher Ideas Press, 1994.

Web Sites

Aaron Shepard's RT Page. http://www.aaronshep.com/rt/index.html
How to use readers theatre, sample scripts from a children's author who specializes in readers theatre, and an extensive list of resources.

Herb and Lois Walker's Scripts for Schools. http://www.scriptsfor schools.com/
Scripts for Schools has more than 100 different scripts for classroom productions in a variety of areas. The scripts are categorized into several different reading levels and are useful in a host of curricular areas.

Reader's Theater Scripts. http://www.geocities.com/EnchantedForest/Tower/3235/index.html
This site has a wide variety of readers theatre scripts. The scripts are organized according to reading levels.

Storycart® Press. http://www.storycart.com

Storycart Press's subscription service provides an inexpensive opportunity to have timely scripts delivered to teachers each month. Each script is created or adapted by well-known writer Suzanne Barchers, author of several readers theatre books (see above). This site also offers a handful of free scripts.

Storytelling, Drama, Creative Dramatics, Puppetry & Readers Theater for Children & Young Adults. http://falcon.jmu.edu/~ramseyil/drama.htm

This site has an incredible listing of storytelling, drama, creative dramatics, and readers theatre scripts for every classroom teacher. There are lots of links and lots of ideas at this all-inclusive site.

Tony is a nationally recognized children's author well known for his energetic, fast-paced, and highly motivating presentations and assemblies at schools across the country. His dynamic and entertaining school visits have captivated thousands of elementary students from coast to coast and border to border—all with rave reviews! His background includes extensive experience as a classroom teacher, curriculum coordinator, staff developer, author, professional storyteller, and university specialist in children's literature and reading methods.

Tony has written more than 50 teacher resource books in a variety of areas, including the hilarious *Tadpole Tales and Other Totally Terrific Treats for Readers Theatre* (Teacher Ideas Press), the award-winning *Guided Reading in Grades 3–6* (Rigby), the best-selling *The Complete Guide to Thematic Units: Creating the Integrated Curriculum* (Christopher-Gordon), and the celebrated *Frantic Frogs and Other Frankly Fractured Folktales for Readers Theatre* (Teacher Ideas Press).

Not only is Tony an advocate for the integration of storytelling and children's literature throughout the curriculum, he is also the author of more than 20 highly acclaimed children's books including *Under One Rock* (Dawn Publications), which was cited by *Skipping Stones* magazine as one of the best books for 2001 in the category of Ecology and Nature; *Slugs* (Lerner), which received an award from the National Science Teachers Association as one of the best nonfiction books in 2000; *Tsunami Man: Learning About Killer Waves with Walter Dudley* (University of Hawaii Press); *Bloodsucking Creatures* (Watts/Scholastic); *Clever Camouflagers* (NorthWord); and *In One Tidepool* (Dawn Publications).

Tony is a professor of education at York College in York, Pennsylvania, where he teaches elementary methods courses in reading, language arts, science, and social studies. Additionally, he maintains a children's author Web site at http://www.afredericks .com, which provides a host of information about his teacher resource books, children's books, and school visits.